S0-BYJ-267

second edition

ANALYTICAL MARKETING EXERCISES

SAM V. SMITH

University of Houston

PRENTICE-HALL, Englewood Cliffs, New Jersey 07632

Library of Congress Cataloging-in-Publication Data

Smith, Sam V.
   Analytical marketing exercises.

   1. Marketing--Problems, exercises, etc.
I. Title.
HF5415.S65 1985   658.8'0076   85-25755
ISBN 0-13-034562-8

Editorial/production supervision: Linda Marie Scardelis
Cover design: Lorraine Mullaney
Manufacturing buyer: Ed O'Dougherty

©1986 by Prentice-Hall
A Division of Simon & Schuster, Inc.
Englewood Cliffs, New Jersey 07632

All rights reserved. No part of this book may be
reproduced, in any form or by any means,
without permission in writing from the publisher.

Printed in the United States of America

 10 9 8 7 6 5 4 3 2 1

   ISBN: 0-13-034562-8 01

Prentice-Hall International (UK) Limited, London
Prentice-Hall of Australia Pty. Limited, Sydney
Prentice-Hall Canada Inc., Toronto
Prentice-Hall Hispanoamericana, S.A., Mexico
Prentice-Hall of India Private Limited, New Delhi
Prentice-Hall of Japan, Inc., Tokyo
Prentice-Hall of Southeast Asia Pte. Ltd., Singapore
Editora Prentice-Hall do Brasil, Ltda., Rio de Janeiro
Whitehall Books Limited, Wellington, New Zealand

CONTENTS

PREFACE

This book was written to help improve the teaching of marketing. Specifically, the purpose is to improve the student's analytical skill. Skill can be developed best by practice in application. Prior to the appearance of this book in its first edition form, marketing instructors teaching the marketing principles course were limited in their choice of pedagogic aids designed to develop analytical skill. With this second edition, I continue the thrust of that earlier publication aimed at providing material to improve student performance. This edition provides a choice of our 100 exercises that can be utilized either as in-class or out-of-class assignments.

The text has been repositioned to reflect the order of the chapters in the third edition of Philip Kotler's <u>Principles of Marketing</u>. Adopters of the Kotler textbook will find my publication will repeat the terminology of the Kotler concepts and principles. These concepts and principles are presented in a variety of real-life settings. Students can demonstrate their individual degrees of understanding of these concepts by their performances on the exercises. In response to requests by users, answers to one-third of the exercises are printed within the book. The student can work through those exercises and immediately obtain feedback on his/her accuracy by referring to the correct answers in the back of this publication.

I wish to give thanks to the many who have contributed ideas to this volume. They include my colleagues at the University of Houston: Gabriel Brehal, Edward A. Blair, Betsy D. Gelb, Michael R. Hyman, Aydin Muderrisoglu, Bette A. Stead, and George M. Zinkhan. Individuals at other universities used the book in its first edition and contributed improvements. They include Karen F. Fox at the University of Santa Clara, William C. Green at North Texas State University, M. L. Klein at California State Polytechnic University, Brian Mohler at Washington State University, Yvonne Petrella at the State University of New York at Oswego, and David R. Rink at Northern Illinois University.

Two secretaries who were very much involved in the preparation of the manuscript are Hermia Bhola and Rachel Berner. Anyone who has worked with Prentice-Hall is aware of the significant contribution of that firm's past and present editors. John M. Connolly contributed to the idea of the volume and Elizabeth Classon helped move it from an idea to reality. Gert Glassen provided assistance in helping me meet deadlines.

I want to give special acknowledgement to Keith Cox who worked with me on the first edition and brought so much of his enthusiasm, insight, and fresh ideas to our joint effort. Unfortunately, other publishing commitments prevent his name from appearing on this second edition but many of the exercises are based on his contributions.

I also wish to express my debt to my family members who were understanding and supportive when the preparation of this volume conflicted with home responsibilities.

Sam V. Smith
University of Houston

INTRODUCTION

Purpose of this Exercise Book

This is a supplement to Philip Kotler's textbook, _Principles of Marketing_, Third Edition. This is an exercise book designed to assist the students in 1) learning the principles and concepts of the introductory marketing course, and 2) developing the skill to be able to apply those principles and concepts to real-life situations.

Basically, this book identifies essential analytical aspects of marketing and offers a set of exercises for each. These exercises provide a novel and efficient method for furthering the student's degree of understanding of those aspects. Thirty-three basic concepts are featured in this book and are listed in the table of contents. Each exercise is keyed to chapters in Kotler's _Principles of Marketing_. Each concept is summarized at the start of each exercise page. Users have a choice of three exercises on each concept.

Major business sources utilized in gathering real examples for the exercises include _Business Week_, _The Wall Street Journal_, _Advertising Age_, _Fortune_, _Forbes_, and a number of major metropolitan newspapers.

Multiple Uses of This Book

This book can be used in a variety of ways.

1. The concepts and examples presented serve the student as a _reinforcing instrument_ to isolate and highlight the essential concepts of the course resulting in the greater learning and understanding that comes from reinforcement.

2. Because the material is printed in a convenient one-page, tear-out form, the instructor has a formal, _feedback_ device that can be turned in by the student and graded quickly by an aide who need not be familiar with the course content. This provides quick feedback to the instructor on the level of comprehension.

3. The student can use the manual as a _learning_ device. One-third of the answers are printed in the book so that the student can measure his or her own degree of comprehension.

But the above are only three uses of the book. Because the material is presented in the form of analytical exercises, those instructors who would like to utilize short case problems can bring to the introductory class this development of analytical skill. So we add the following uses of this book:

4. The instructor has an alternative to the use of short cases as a basis for _developing discussion_ on the application of course concepts to problem situations. From the discussion, the instructor also has an informal, immediate feedback of the level of understanding of the basic concepts of the course.

5. Because the exercises are short, discussion of the problems in a large classroom can occur <u>without assignment prior</u> to the class. The students can read the exercise in class and work them in class.

Instructors who have had experience in meeting the responsibilities of the introductory class (where non-marketing majors outnumber the students who are planning to major in marketing) know the value of a change of pace to maintain student involvement. Because the exercise book is light in weight, it can be conveniently carried to each class for quick use.

6. The exercise book provides the instructor with this <u>change of pace</u> without the need for prior preparation and distribution of expensive hand-out material.

Because of the vast amount of material that must be covered by the typical introductory marketing textbook, authors are limited in the number of examples they can present. To correct this, we offer the following:

7. The student is asked to apply the concept in a wide variety of <u>real-life situations</u>. In the process, the student develops the ability to deal with situations that may include an industrial marketer, a service operation or a not-for-profit organization.

ANALYTICAL MARKETING EXERCISES

PART ONE

Understanding Marketing

This section starts with the fundamental question of how does the organization conduct its exchange relationships. Managers must choose from the alternative marketing management philosophies of the production concept, the product concept, the selling concept, or the marketing concept. Next, what growth strategies exist and how are they followed in actual practice. This requires the student to be able to differentiate among market penetration, market development, and product development strategies.

The third part of this section acquaints the student with real-life examples of managers developing marketing mix programs. The first exercise in this set requires the student to identify the structure of the marketing program for a retailer. The second one is a for-profit service organization and the third illustrates marketing mix planning in an educational institution.

© 1986 by Prentice-Hall, A Division of Simon & Schuster, Inc.
Englewood Cliffs, N.J. 07632. All rights reserved.
Printed in the United States of America.

Exercise 1-1   MARKETING MANAGEMENT PHILOSOPHIES

Four traditional major alternative philosophies under which firms can conduct their marketing plans and activities are 1) production, 2) product, 3) selling, and 4) marketing. One of the oldest philosophies is the production concept which assumes that the major task of management is to improve production and distribution efficiency. Therefore, the role of marketing, under the production concept, is to facilitate the efficient manufacturing and distribution of the firm's products or services. A second philosophy is the product concept which assumes that buyers will respond most to improvements in product performance, quality or features. In contrast, the selling concept maintains that customers are quite reluctant to exchange their funds for a firm's products or services therefore the role of marketing is aggressively to promote and sell the firm's offerings. The marketing concept assumes that the first major responsibility of management is to determine the needs and wants of target markets. Accordingly, the role of marketing is to satisfy those needs and wants better than one's competitors.

> Instructions: Read each of the following statements and indicate which concept is involved. Select just one concept for each sentence. (For purposes of simplifying the format of this first assignment, the societal marketing concept is omitted.)

	Production Concept	Product Concept	Selling Concept	Marketing Concept
1. The Chicago Driver's License Bureau processes new and renewal licenses each year. Although long lines of applicants are frequent, the bureau is highly efficient in processing applicants.	( )	( )	( )	( )
2. Exxon conducted a six-month test of First City bank-teller cards at ten Houston-area stations. Machines, similar to a bank's electronic tellers, were installed at the pumps. The system was designed to reduce manpower needs at the stations and, hopefully, be a convenience to customers.	( )	( )	( )	( )
3. Forest Lawn, a large funeral chain, sells prepaid funeral services in addition to its regular funeral services. Since many people are reluctant to buy funeral services	( )	( )	( )	( )

© 1986 by Prentice-Hall, A Division of Simon & Schuster, Inc.
Englewood Cliffs, N.J. 07632. All rights reserved.
Printed in the United States of America.

	Production Concept	Product Concept	Selling Concept	Marketing Concept
before they are needed, salespeople for Forest Lawn must energetically push their prepaid funeral services.				
4. Kroger supermarkets are strong in the Midwest and South. Its president said that the fundamental strength of Kroger lies in "listening to what customers are telling us."	( )	( )	( )	( )
5. Munsingwear, a clothing manufacturer with products such as Penguin shirts and Vassarette lingerie, emphasizes the high quality of its clothing products.	( )	( )	( )	( )
6. American Telephone and Telegraph (AT&T) is a giant utility firm. It has pioneered new technology in the communication industry and has concentrated on improved telephone operations.	( )	( )	( )	( )
7. Many political candidates of both the Democratic and Republican parties assume that people will not vote for them without substantial advertising and personal appearances.	( )	( )	( )	( )
8. Francis Coppola, turbulent Hollywood director, claimed "marketing is a word which singlehandedly destroyed Detroit." He stated that the right way to design toasters is to build the best toaster you can make.	( )	( )	( )	( )
9. Braniff Airlines, upon its initial reorganization after bankruptcy, offered meals served to its passengers on china rather than plastic trays. Customer traffic did not significantly increase.	( )	( )	( )	( )
10. Walt Disney has helped to pioneer and expand the entertainment market. Disney has always adapted its services to customers interested in good entertainment.	( )	( )	( )	( )

Exercise 1-2   MARKETING MANAGEMENT PHILOSOPHIES

   Four traditional major alternative philosophies under which firms can
conduct their marketing plans and activities are 1) production, 2) product,
3) selling, and 4) marketing. One of the oldest philosophies is the <u>pro-
duction concept</u> which assumes that the major task of management is to
improve production and distribution efficiency. Therefore, the role of
marketing, under the production concept, is to facilitate the efficient
manufacturing and distribution of the firm's products or services. A
secondary philosophy is the <u>product concept</u>, which assumes that buyers will
respond most to improvements in product performance, quality, or features.
In contrast, the <u>selling concept</u> maintains that customers are quite reluctant to exchange their funds for a firm's products or services therefore
the role of marketing is aggressively to promote and sell the firm's offerings. The <u>marketing concept</u> assumes that the first major responsibility of
management is to determine the needs and wants of target markets. Accordingly, the role of marketing is to satisfy those needs and wants better than
one's competitors.

          Instructions: Read each of the following statements
          and indicate which concept is involved. Select just
          one concept for each sentence. (For purpose of sim-
          plifying the format of this first assignment, the
          societal marketing concept is omitted.)

		Production Concept	Product Concept	Selling Concept	Marketing Concept
1.	The City of Miami opened its new $1 billion heavy rail transit system in 1984. After six months, average daily ridership was 10% of predicted volume.	( )	( )	( )	( )
2.	Yellow Cab customers who wish to make telephone calls while traveling may request a cab with a telephone if they schedule one day in advance of need. Long distance calls must be charged to a third party or a credit card.	( )	( )	( )	( )
3.	World Book Encyclopedia is considered a leader in its industry. The sales force is trained to present a strong "canned" sales presentation to potential customers.	( )	( )	( )	( )
4.	Texas Instruments is a large	( )	( )	( )	( )

© 1986 by Prentice-Hall, A Division of Simon & Schuster, Inc.
Englewood Cliffs, N.J. 07632. All rights reserved.
Printed in the United States of America.

	Production Concept	Product Concept	Selling Concept	Marketing Concept

integrated electronic firm that sells high-technology products. Employing the learning curve concept to reduce production costs, Texas Instruments uses the expected lower costs to cut prices and expand the market size.

5. Eastman Kodak is a large corporation best known for its Kodak photographic products. The new disc camera was developed after extensive marketing research was done to determine whether potential customers liked the product's proposed features.   ( )   ( )   ( )   ( )

6. To improve availability of service, Control Data Corp., which sells information services through store-front offices known as Control Data Business Centers, opened 120 outlets. CDBC processes data on new large computers.   ( )   ( )   ( )   ( )

7. Control Data failed to anticipate the proliferation of personal computers that reduced demand for the centers' type of service. By the end of 1984, CDBC closed 100 of its 120 Business Centers.   ( )   ( )   ( )   ( )

8. The U.S. Post Office processes a staggering amount of mail each working day. It greatly emphasizes processing the mail more efficiently.   ( )   ( )   ( )   ( )

9. The Horizon Land Development Company sells vacation property to a wide variety of people. Prospects are flown to the vacation property, where the sales force strongly attempt to sell the vacation property utilizing a team selling approach.   ( )   ( )   ( )   ( )

10. Kentucky Fried Chicken was one of the early fast-food franchises. They have catered to a large group of consumers who buy at fast-food franchises because the food does not vary in quality from location to location and the service is acceptable.   ( )   ( )   ( )   ( )

Exercise 1-3   MARKETING MANAGEMENT PHILOSOPHIES

Four traditional major alternative philosophies under which firms can conduct their marketing plans and activities are 1) production, 2) product, 3) selling, and 4) marketing. One of the oldest philosophies is the <u>production concept</u>, which assumes that the major task of management is to improve production and distribution efficiency. Therefore, the role of marketing, under the production concept, is to facilitate the efficient manufacturing and distribution of the firm's products or services. A secondary philosophy is the <u>product concept</u>, which assumes that buyers will respond most to improvements in product performance, quality, or features. In contrast, the <u>selling concept</u> maintains that customers are quite reluctant to exchange their funds for a firm's products or services therefore the role of marketing is aggressively to promote and sell the firm's offerings. The <u>marketing concept</u> assumes that the first major responsibility of management is to determine the needs and wants of target markets. Accordingly, the role of marketing is to satisfy those needs and wants better than one's competitors.

Instructions: Read each of the following statements and indicate which concept is involved. Select just one concept for each sentence. (For purpose of simplifying the format of this first assignment, the societal marketing concept is omitted.)

	Production Concept	Product Concept	Selling Concept	Marketing Concept
1. CompuFund, a computer service firm, offers real-estate agents information about mortgages. Agents can bring their personal computers into houses, plug into phones and tell would-be buyers what loans are available. Many brokers say, as of 1985, the technology offers a very limited view of the mortgage market.	( )	( )	( )	( )
2. General Foods Corp., pleased with market prospects for cereal, developed Crazy Cartons. Crazy Cartons were cereal in half-pint milk cartons. The product was a failure.	( )	( )	( )	( )
3. Most universities attempt to maximize the number of students registered per day in their registration process.	( )	( )	( )	( )

© 1986 by Prentice-Hall, A Division of Simon & Schuster, Inc.
Englewood Cliffs, N.J. 07632. All rights reserved.
Printed in the United States of America.

	Production Concept	Product Concept	Selling Concept	Marketing Concept
4. Steiger Tractor Company manufactures expensive tractors in Fargo, North Dakota, for large farm operations. Steiger has found a highly concentrated market for supertractors in the $120,000-$135,000 price range.	( )	( )	( )	( )
5. Believing that telephone users would like to see the person on the other end of the line, American Telephone & Telegraph Co. developed picture phones as early as 1964. There has been little market response.	( )	( )	( )	( )
6. The Reed Aluminum Siding Company sells aluminum siding to home owners. Because most home owners do not recognize the benefits, the sales force must convince prospects of the value of aluminum siding.	( )	( )	( )	( )
7. Consolidiated Edison is one of the largest electrical utilities in the United States. With its basic costs increasing rapidly, Consolidiated Edison is trying to improve its technology for producing and distributing electricity.	( )	( )	( )	( )
8. General Electric is a large multi national corporation. For years, GE has been a leader in identifying market needs and then developing products to meet these needs.	( )	( )	( )	( )
9. All types of bibles are sold by door-to-door salespeople. Frequently, these bibles are sold by using pressure tactics.	( )	( )	( )	( )
10. Single, freeze-frame pictures transmitted by telephone were utilized by engineers restoring the Statue of Liberty. When they needed advice on a broken or worn part, they telephoned a picture of the part to offices in Manhattan or Paris.	( )	( )	( )	( )

Exercise 2-1   MARKET OPPORTUNITY IDENTIFICATION:
                                  INTENSIVE GROWTH STRATEGIES

Intensive growth strategies, in contrast to external growth strategies, are those growth opportunities available to the firm within its current sphere of operations.

There are three major types of intensive growth strategies: 1) market penetration, 2) market development, and 3) product development. Market penetration involves the firm's trying to increase sales of its present products in its present markets. Getting existing customers to increase usage of the product, converting competitors' customers to the firm's product, and converting nonusers to users are three ways of using a market penetration strategy. Market development involves the firm's trying to increase sales by selling its products in new markets. Expanding into new geographical markets and developing new target markets not currently being served effectively are examples of market development strategy. Product development involves the firm's trying to increase sales by developing new or improved products in existing markets. Two ways of using a product development strategy are to develop new product features and to create different versions of the existing product.

> Instructions: Analyze each of the following statements and indicate which growth strategy is primarily involved. Select only one strategy for each statement.

	Market Penetration	Market Development	Product Development
1. Dayton Hudson, a retailing conglomerate of department stores, discount stores, and book stores, continues to open Target stores in new cities.	( )	( )	( )
2. Equitable Life Insurance Company is one of the largest companies in the insurance industry. It has introduced a new variable life insurance policy to complement its traditional whole-life and term policies.	( )	( )	( )
3. Scripto sells a full line of ball-point pens. Recently, Scripto broadened its product line by developing and introducing a new erasable pen.	( )	( )	( )
4. Philip Morris's leading cigarette brand, Marlboro, continues to increase its sales throughout the world. Marlboro's	( )	( )	( )

© 1986 by Prentice-Hall, A Division of Simon & Schuster, Inc.
Englewood Cliffs, N.J. 07632. All rights reserved.
Printed in the United States of America.

	Market Penetration	Market Development	Product Development

aggressive advertising has helped Marlboro increase its share of the market.

5. Coca-Cola developed and introduced Mr. Pibb as a new soft drink. Mr. Pibb is a brand of carbonated soda water.   ( ) ( ) ( )

6. Arm and Hammer is the leader in the baking soda industry. The firm increased its sales dramatically by advertising the idea of using baking soda in refrigerators to reduce food odors.   ( ) ( ) ( )

7. Merrill Lynch, the largest stockbroker in the United States, has traditionally sold its services to the businessman market. In the late 1970s, Merrill Lynch developed special services for the emerging women's market.   ( ) ( ) ( )

8. Johnson & Johnson has successfully sold Johnson's baby shampoo to the baby market for over 20 years. With the anticipated decline in baby births, Johnson & Johnson has widened its appeal to the adult market, emphasizing that its gentle ingredients allow daily shampooing of users' hair without damage.   ( ) ( ) ( )

9. Dow Chemical company sells Dowgard antifreeze for automobiles. One advertising campaign was aimed at persuading customers to change their antifreeze more frequently.   ( ) ( ) ( )

10. Atari, a firm that had been the leader in the video game market, tried to offset falling sales by expanding its distribution through the installation of its consoles and game cartridges in country clubs and hotels.   ( ) ( ) ( )

11. Atari also designed and attempted to sell home computers that could be used in playing Atari video games when sales of its original product line declined.   ( ) ( ) ( )

12. In a vain effort to correct the industry decline in video cartridge games, Atari spent more than $75 million advertising its existing product line in 1982.   ( ) ( ) ( )

10

Exercise 2-2   MARKET OPPORTUNITY IDENTIFICATION:
                                INTENSIVE GROWTH STRATEGIES

Intensive growth strategies, in contrast to external growth strategies, are those growth opportunities available to the firm within its current sphere of operations.

There are three major types of intensive growth strategies: 1) market penetration, 2) market development, and 3) product development. Market penetration involves the firm's trying to increase sales of its present products in its present markets. Getting existing customers to increase usage of the product, converting competitors' customers to the firm's product, and converting nonusers to users are three ways of using a market penetration strategy. Market development involves the firm's trying to increase sales by selling its products in new markets. Expanding into new geographical markets and developing new target markets not currently being served effectively are examples of market development strategy. Product development involves the firm's trying to increase sales by developing new or improved products in existing markets. Two ways of using a product development strategy are to develop new product features and to create different versions of the existing product.

Instructions: Analyze each of the following statements and indicate which growth strategy is primarily involved. Select only one strategy for each statement.

	Market Penetration	Market Development	Product Development
1. A 20% discount card has been made available to transit riders who use the bus at least ten times a month.	( )	( )	( )
2. Twenty new minibuses were purchased by the public transit company. These minibuses will run exclusively in the existing central business district.	( )	( )	( )
3. By increasing the frequency of bus service during the morning and evening rush hours, the public transit company hopes to increase ridership.	( )	( )	( )
4. The public transit company announced that it will be extending its bus service to five small cities close to the large metropolitan city.	( )	( )	( )

© 1986 by Prentice-Hall, A Division of Simon & Schuster, Inc.
Englewood Cliffs, N.J. 07632. All rights reserved.
Printed in the United States of America.

11

	Market Penetration	Market Development	Product Development
5. A new advertising campaign is aimed at people not currently using the transit buses. Management hopes that awareness of the transit company will lead to an increase in bus riders.	( )	( )	( )
6. The public transit company decided to expand its customer base by selling to the convention market. It converted some existing buses to charter buses for the convention market.	( )	( )	( )
7. The public transit company has bought 50 new and improved buses. These new buses have a 30% greater rider capacity than the existing buses in use.	( )	( )	( )
8. The public transit company has committed a billion dollar contract to build a new subway system. This system will replace a portion of the existing bus lines.	( )	( )	( )
9. The public transit company arranged for restricted traffic lanes to be built in the centers of the two major highways leading into the city. Only buses were permitted on these lanes.	( )	( )	( )
10. Several buses were designated for handicapped riders. Prior to this, handicapped individuals had to rely either on privately maintained vehicles or, in the case of school children, special routes.	( )	( )	( )
11. Land was purchased by the transit company to be converted to parking lots for private vehicles so that transit riders could drive from their homes in their private cars to convenient gathering points. There, riders could get on the buses for the remainder of their trip to town.	( )	( )	( )

Exercise 2-3

MARKET OPPORTUNITY IDENTIFICATION:
INTENSIVE GROWTH STRATEGIES

Intensive growth strategies, in contrast to external growth strategies, are those growth opportunities available to the firm within its
current sphere of operations.

There are three major types of intensive growth strategies: 1) market
penetration, 2) market development, and 3) product development. Market
penetration involves the firm's trying to increase sales of its present
products in its present markets. Getting existing customers to increase
usage of the product, converting competitors' customers to the firm's
product, and converting nonusers to users are three ways of using a market
penetration strategy. Market development involves the firm's trying to
increase sales by selling its products in new markets. Expanding into new
geographical markets and developing new target markets not currently being
served effectively are examples of market development strategy. Product
development involves the firm's trying to increase sales by developing new
or improved products in existing markets. Two ways of using a product development strategy are to develop new product features and to create different versions of the existing product.

Instructions: Analyze each of the following statements
and indicate which growth strategy is primarily involved. Select only one strategy for each statement.

	Market Penetration	Market Development	Product Development
1. Levi Strauss International successfully introduced its blue jeans to the Japanese market. By 1977, sales of Levi Strauss International alone totaled $518 million.	( )	( )	( )
2. Levi Strauss developed a new line of jeans called Mr. Levi's. This new line was developed to appeal to the existing male market as men grew older.	( )	( )	( )
3. Radio advertisements are used by Levi Strauss to obtain additional teenage impact for the back-to-school promotions in July and August.	( )	( )	( )
4. With rapid acceptance of fashion in male leisure clothes, Levi Strauss created a new men's sportswear division in 1971, offering three types of casual clothes.	( )	( )	( )

© 1986 by Prentice-Hall, A Division of Simon & Schuster, Inc.
Englewood Cliffs, N.J. 07632. All rights reserved.
Printed in the United States of America.

	Market Penetration	Market Development	Product Development
5. Levi Strauss' share of the jean market fell from 50% to 30% in the late 1970s, primarily due to the demand for designer jeans. Levi Strauss responded by reducing their prices.	( )	( )	( )
6. In the 1950s, Levi Strauss introduced Levi's Lighter Blue, which became the highly successful faded blue denim jean.	( )	( )	( )
7. As the blue jeans industry has matured, Levi Strauss has tried to get additional business from their competition by increasing the number of retail stores carrying their blue jeans. Both Sears and Penney's started carrying Levi's blue jeans in 1981. Neither chain had been permitted to stock Levi's prior to that time.	( )	( )	( )
8. In 1969, Levi Strauss entered the European market. The existing products were produced in European plants purchased by Levi Strauss.	( )	( )	( )
9. Some executives at Levi Strauss debated the wisdom of the firm's opening factory outlets where not only irregular merchandise but also surplus goods could be sold for an attractive margin.	( )	( )	( )
10. Sears added Levi's to its line because Sears wanted a broader assortment of sportswear to complement its own lines. Sears already had a budget line of Rough-Houser children's pants, a better line of Toughskins. Levi's, priced above Toughskins, round out the assortment.	( )	( )	( )
11. Observing that Levi's blue jeans had probably reached its peak of popularity, Levi's executives introduced a line of suits. Required alterations were reduced by selling the pants separately from the coats.	( )	( )	( )

Exercise 3-1   THE MARKETING MIX DECISION

   A marketing manager has to cope with both controllable and uncontrollable factors in planning the marketing program. The marketing mix is the
particular blend of controllable marketing variables that the manager puts
together to satisfy the needs of target markets. The endless variety of
variables can be collected into four submixes that are known as the "four
P's": 1) product, 2) price, 3) place, and 4) promotion. <u>Product</u> consists
of all the decisions directly affecting the specific product or service
being offered to the target market. It includes the products offered,
quality, packaging, brands, and related services. <u>Price</u> refers to the actual
price selected, discounts, allowances, payment plans, and credit terms.
<u>Place</u> consists of decisions regarding the place where the item being of-
fered can be purchased, the type of channels selected, the intensity of
distribution, and the transportation and storage of the product. <u>Promotion</u>
includes decisions regarding advertising, personal selling, sales promotion,
and publicity.

   The Blackwelder Furniture Company in Statesville, North Carolina, sells
top-line brand-name furniture at a discount price throughout the southern
United States.

          Instructions: Read each of the following statements and
          indicate which submix or group of variables is primarily
          involved. Select just one group for each statement.

		Product	Price	Place	Promotion
1.	Blackwelder sells luxurious Henredon brand sofas.	( )	( )	( )	( )
2.	Blackwelder mails batches of manufac- turers' catalogs, showing what is available in particular lines and styles, to inquiring customers.	( )	( )	( )	( )
3.	Markups for name furniture average 35% of cost at Blackwelder, while the usual furniture markup at furniture stores is at least 100% of cost.	( )	( )	( )	( )
4.	Blackwelder will deliver a sofa more than 350 miles to an Atlanta home and set it up in the living room.	( )	( )	( )	( )
5.	Using an 800 toll-free number, sizable business sales are completed over the phone from Atlanta.	( )	( )	( )	( )
6.	No house brands are carried by Blackwelder.	( )	( )	( )	( )

© 1986 by Prentice-Hall, A Division of Simon & Schuster, Inc.
Englewood Cliffs, N.J. 07632. All rights reserved.
Printed in the United States of America.

15

	Product	Price	Place	Promotion
7. Since Blackwelder is located close to most of the major furniture manufacturers, the company does not maintain extensive warehousing of furniture.	( )	( )	( )	( )
8. In Statesville, Blackwelder operates a 5,700-square-foot retail store.	( )	( )	( )	( )
9. According to the head of the Southern Home Furnisher Association, "Blackwelder is raising hell in the industry and messing up the price structure."	( )	( )	( )	( )
10. Blackwelder executives considered reducing the price on all orders that were prepaid two weeks prior to shipment.	( )	( )	( )	( )
11. To increase sales in what had traditionally been a poor month, management debated offering a lounge chair free with certain sofa purchases.	( )	( )	( )	( )
12. The bookstore manager at a major state university suggested to Blackwelder management that it provide copies of its catalog s to college bookstores for use by faculty.	( )	( )	( )	( )
13. Blackwelder executives were not disturbed by their trade association's criticism of Blackwelder's procedures.	( )	( )	( )	( )
14. Some of the Blackwelder executives were considering expanding into the southwestern United States.	( )	( )	( )	( )
15. Expansion into the Southwest would require buyers to pay larger delivery charges, reducing Blackwelder's advantages over competition.	( )	( )	( )	( )

Exercise 3-2   THE MARKETING-MIX DECISION

A marketing manager has to cope with both controllable and uncontrollable factors in planning the marketing program. The marketing mix is the particular blend of controllable marketing variables that the manager puts together to satisfy the needs of target markets. The endless variety of variables can be collected into four submixes that are known as the "four P's": 1) product, 2) price, 3) place, and 4) promotion. <u>Product</u> consists of all the decisions directly affecting the specific product or service being offered to the target market. It includes the products offered, quality, packaging, brands, and related services. <u>Price</u> refers to the actual price selected, discounts, allowances, payment plans, and credit terms. <u>Place</u> consists of decisions regarding the place where the item being offered can be purchased, the type of channels selected, the intensity of distribution, and the transportation and storage of the product. <u>Promotion</u> includes decisions regarding advertising, personal selling, sales promotion, and publicity.

Bekins Van Lines Company is a Los Angeles-based moving firm that specializes in household moving. The combination of deregulation of the household moving industry and a weak housing market has caused major changes in the industry.

Instructions: Read each of the following statements and indicate which submix or group of variables is primarily involved. Select just one group for each statement.

		<u>Product</u>	<u>Price</u>	<u>Place</u>	<u>Promotion</u>
1.	The sales force for the Bekins Van Lines Company is given three-day refresher sales training courses each year.	( )	( )	( )	( )
2.	Bekins has expanded its delivery to all geographical areas within the United States.	( )	( )	( )	( )
3.	In the current year, Bekins has placed color advertisements in most major women's magazines.	( )	( )	( )	( )
4.	Twenty new distributors have been added by Bekins in the last five years.	( )	( )	( )	( )
5.	Bekins now offers insurance to cover the full replacement cost of damaged goods.	( )	( )	( )	( )

© 1986 by Prentice-Hall, A Division of Simon & Schuster, Inc.
Englewood Cliffs, N.J. 07632. All rights reserved.
Printed in the United States of America.

	Product	Price	Place	Promotion
6. An 8% discount is given to customers who pay their moving bill in advance.	( )	( )	( )	( )
7. Bekins now gives binding cost estimates to all customers.	( )	( )	( )	( )
8. A new service started this year by Bekins is to guarantee to customers the pickup and delivery date.	( )	( )	( )	( )
9. A special moving service for large business and government customers is used by Bekins.	( )	( )	( )	( )
10. A cluster of brochures has been developed by Bekins that profile basic services in the customer's new communities.	( )	( )	( )	( )
11. Bekins offers special handling for electronic equipment such as computers.	( )	( )	( )	( )
12. Bekins will provide spouse re-employment assistance in the new community through its local offices.	( )	( )	( )	( )
13. To assist the customer planning a move, Bekins provides free a sheet that lists local services that must be terminated, such as newspaper delivery, electricity, mail, etc.	( )	( )	( )	( )
14. The same rate is charged for day or night moving and for each of the seven days of the week.	( )	( )	( )	( )
15. Bekins gives a printed publication to all prospects that compares Bekins' performance records with five other moving firms. The data are reprinted from Interstate Commerce Commission reports.	( )	( )	( )	( )

Exercise 3-3   THE MARKETING-MIX DECISION

A marketing manager has to cope with both controllable and uncontrollable factors in planning the marketing program. The marketing mix is the particular blend of controllable marketing variables that the manager puts together to satisfy the needs of target markets. The endless variety of variables can be collected into four submixes that are known as the "four P's": 1) product, 2) price, 3) place, and 4) promotion. Product consists of all the decisions directly affecting the specific product or service being offered to the target market. It includes the products offered, quality, packaging, brands, and related services. Price refers to the actual price selected, discounts, allowances, payment plans, and credit terms. Place consists of decisions regarding the place where the item being offered can be purchased, the type of channels selected, the intensity of distribution, and the transportation and storage of the product. Promotion includes decisions regarding advertising, personal selling, sales promotion, and publicity.

Hood College, an independent liberal arts college for women located in Frederick, Maryland, was founded in 1898.

Instructions: Read each of the following statements and indicate which submix or group of variables is primarily involved. Select just one group for each statement.

	Product	Price	Place	Promotion
1. In 1915, the education department was formed in response to the need for college-trained teachers.	( )	( )	( )	( )
2. In 1973, the board of trustees developed a series of educational programs incorporating a strong liberal-arts core.	( )	( )	( )	( )
3. The admissions staff developed a free 32-page publication describing the departments at Hood.	( )	( )	( )	( )
4. In the early 1970's the cost of attending Hood College was consistently below that of similar institutions.	( )	( )	( )	( )
5. A new logo was designed using the name of the college with the second "o" printed to look like the universal female symbol.	( )	( )	( )	( )
6. The board of trustees considered	( )	( )	( )	( )

© 1986 by Prentice-Hall, A Division of Simon & Schuster, Inc.
Englewood Cliffs, N.J. 07632. All rights reserved.
Printed in the United States of America.

offering existing courses off-
campus, in Baltimore and Washington.

7. Internship programs were developed   ( )   ( )   ( )   ( )
    in a variety of occupations, in-
    cluding work in the health science
    field.

8. College administrators offer quali-   ( )   ( )   ( )   ( )
    fied students a loan program not
    requiring repayments until after
    graduation.

9. The scheduling of existing classes   ( )   ( )   ( )   ( )
    was revised to offer greater con-
    venience for students by having
    all health science classes in one
    building.

10. Several newspaper articles in the   ( )   ( )   ( )   ( )
    Washington Post and the Baltimore
    Sun described the success of Hood
    College in increasing applications
    at a time when other private
    schools were reporting declines.

11. From its beginnings, Hood College   ( )   ( )   ( )   ( )
    sought to provide quality educa-
    tion exclusively for women.

12. The board of trustees considered   ( )   ( )   ( )   ( )
    utilizing an educational televi-
    sion channel to reach off-campus
    students in the nearby Maryland-
    Virginia viewing area.

13. The role of the college chaplain   ( )   ( )   ( )   ( )
    was redefined so that half of his
    time was allocated to serving as
    a counselor for older, commuting
    students.

14. Several prominent local business   ( )   ( )   ( )   ( )
    organizations were asked to con-
    sider establishing tuition-
    reimbursement programs for
    employees taking evening classes
    at the college.

Source: Some of this information is drawn from E. Raymond Corey,
         Christopher H. Lovelock, and Scott Ward, Problems in
         Marketing, Sixth Edition (New York: McGraw-Hill, 1981),
         pp. 46-61.

PART TWO

Organizing the Marketing Planning Process

This section looks at how marketing activities are created and integrated under the organization's overall strategic plan. Strategic planning involves the identification of strategic business units (SBU's) and the analysis of relevant opportunities and threats to each unit. The first set of exercises in this section requires the student to demonstrate an understanding of business portfolio analysis and SBU's. Three situations dealing with the Boston Consulting Group's (BCG's) matrix approach to portfolio analysis appear. The first exercise presents real data from the Procter & Gamble Company. The second situation reflects the highly dynamic soft-drink industry and illustrates the importance of understanding the market segments in the industry. The third is an update of a popular exercise from the first edition of this book: the Gillette Company. This third situation concentrates on competition between Gillette and Bic. There is opportunity here to discuss in class alternative strategies for low-growth products and to compare them with Gillette's action with regard to its Cricket brand of cigarette lighters. This discussion naturally leads into the external growth strategies of backward, forward, and horizontal integration.

The final set of exercises in this section assists the student in understanding the structured, interacting complex of persons, equipment, and procedures that constitutes the marketing information system. Here the student will see how the subsystems of internal reports, marketing intelligence, marketing research, and analytical marketing combine to provide an orderly flow of information to aid decision makers. The student must identify each of these subsystems in operations that range from industrial and consumer goods manufacturers to services such as the well-known 911 emergency telephone number.

© 1986 by Prentice-Hall, A Division of Simon & Schuster, Inc.
Englewood Cliffs, N.J. 07632. All rights reserved.
Printed in the United States of America.

Exercise 4-1   BUSINESS PORTFOLIO ANALYSIS

Procter & Gamble Co. (P&G) is headquartered in Cincinnati, Ohio. P&G, the nation's largest advertiser, is a giant firm with a wide variety of household products. Some of its products were developed internally by this 148 year-old firm. Others were obtained through acquisitions. In recent years, it has lost position in certain significant product markets where it once was dominant, but market analysts expect P&G to rebound with vigor.

Toothpaste

In terms of market position, P&G dropped to a 31% share of market in 1984 with its Crest brand. Total industry sales exceeded $1 billion. Colgate, a product of Colgate-Palmolive Co., recently moved to a strong second place 28% share with the aid of its innovative pump package. Other brands follow with smaller shares. The toothpaste annual market growth rate is estimated to be 8%.

Disposable-Diapers

Total industry sales of disposable diapers reached $2.5 billion in 1984. Kimberly-Clark Corp.'s Huggies brand have been gaining market share at P&G's expense. K&C's Huggies had a 32% share of market in 1984. P&G's standard brand Pampers that at one time had a share greater than 50% fell to 30%. P&G's premium brand Luvs was at 16% in 1984, also a record low. P&G plans to introduce improved versions of both brands in 1985.

General Laundry Detergent

P&G's Tide is the biggest seller in the laundry detergent category with a 22% market share, down three percentage points from 1981. Unilever's Wisk was in second place at an 8% market share in 1983. All, also produced by Unilever, held a 5% market share. The market growth rate is thought to be 4%.

© 1986 by Prentice-Hall, A Division of Simon & Schuster, Inc.
Englewood Cliffs, N.J. 07632. All rights reserved.
Printed in the United States of America.   23

The BCG Portfolio Matrix

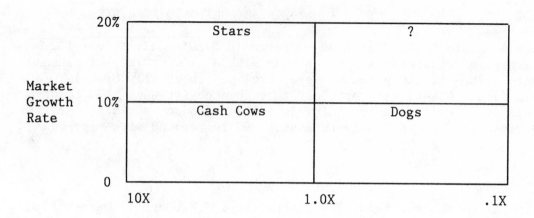

Relative Market Share

$$\text{Relative Market Share} = \frac{\text{Our Company's Share of Market}}{\text{Leading Competitor's Share of Market}}$$

Place the following three circles of P&G products in their proper positions within the BCG product portfolio matrix:

   P&G's Crest toothpaste brand - C

   P&G's disposable diaper brand Pampers - P

   P&G's disposable diaper brand Luvs - L

   P&G's Tide laundry detergent - T

Exercise 4-2   BUSINESS-PORTFOLIO ANALYSIS

In the U.S. soft drink industry, where 1% of the market is worth $300 million in retail sales, Coca-Cola Co. and PepsiCo are engaged in all-out war. The Coca-Cola Co., headquartered in Atlanta, Georgia, made worldwide news in 1985 when it changed its secret, 100 year-old formula for Coke. PepsiCo proudly claimed responsibility for the change saying that its Pepsi challenge advertising campaign was responsible for Coke's modification.

Traditional Cola Drinks

Coca-Cola Co.'s basic Coke brand remained the industry leader at 40.1% share of market for 1984. Pepsi Cola was a close second at 30.1%. The growth rate of the traditional cola market has slowed to about 5%. For the first time, cola drinks account for less than 60% of the soft drink market.

Diet Cola Drinks

One of the most successful new product introductions in recent years is Diet Coke. By 1984, it had 40% of the diet cola market. Diet Pepsi was in second place with 25% with a variety of regional and local brands fighting with Coca-Cola Co.'s Tab for the rest of the market. With baby-boomers showing a growing dislike for high calorie soft drinks, the diet soft drink market is growing at a 12% growth rate.

Lemon-Lime and Fruit Juice-Added Drinks

Seven-Up currently leads this category. In 1984, its market share was 34.8%. Coca-Cola Co.'s Sprite was in second place at 21.9%. Slice, introduced in test markets that year by PepsiCo was expected to be third at a 19.9% share of market. The market for lemon-lime and fruit juice-added drinks has an attractive growth rate of 10%.

© 1986 by Prentice-Hall, A Division of Simon & Schuster, Inc.
Englewood Cliffs, N.J. 07632. All rights reserved.
Printed in the United States of America.

The BCG Portfolio Matrix

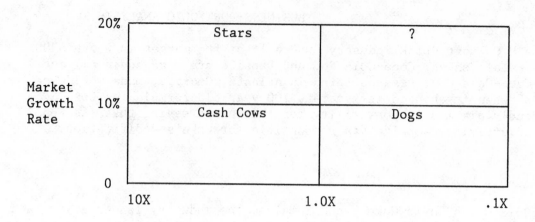

$$\text{Relative Market Share} = \frac{\text{Our Company's Share of Market}}{\text{Leading Competitor's Share of Market}}$$

Place the following circles of Coca-Cola Co. and PepsiCo products in their proper positions within the product portfolio matrix.

Traditional Cola Market

        Coca-Cola Co.'s Coke   CC

        PepsiCo's Pepsi Cola   PC

Diet Cola Market

        Coca Cola Co.'s Diet Coke   DC

        PepsiCo's Diet Pepsi   DP

Lemon-Lime Market

        Coca Cola Co.'s Sprite   CS

        PepsiCo's Slice   PS

Exercise 4-3   BUSINESS PORTFOLIO ANALYSIS

The Gillette Company and Bic Corp. had been competing head-to-head with three products: 1) disposable ballpoint pens, 2) disposable lighters, and 3) disposable razors.

Razors

Gillette has dominated the razor market for decades, and presently has a 58% share of market. Schick follows with a 20% share, with Bic in third place with 15%. Bic has concentrated on the lower end of the razor market with its disposable Bic razor. Gillette has introduced its Good News disposable razor to compete directly with Bic. With the decline in population growth, the razor blade market is basically a low growth market with an estimated 2% growth rate.

Lighters

One year after Gillette introduced its Cricket brand of lighters, Bic introduced its own lighter. Bic ran a flashy "Flick My Bic" advertising campaign for a number of years. Bic slashed the price of its lighter by 32 percent in 1977, and a price war ensued between Bic and Gillette. Today, Bic has a 54% share of market in the lighter market, while Cricket has dropped to 16%. Industry experts estimate an 8% growth rate through the 1980s.

Ballpoint Pens

Bic invaded the U.S. market in the early 1960s with its cheap ballpoint pens. Gillette's Papermate did not introduce its own line of low-priced pens until 1972. Gillette has recently introduced its Write Bros. pens to compete more directly with Bic. Presently, Bic has a 60% share of market while Gillette trails with a 25% share. With an estimated 10% growth rate for ballpoint pens, Bic is fighting hard to keep its traditional dominance in the pen industry.

© 1986 by Prentice-Hall, A Division of Simon & Schuster, Inc.
Englewood Cliffs, N.J. 07632. All rights reserved.
Printed in the United States of America.

The BCG Portfolio Matrix

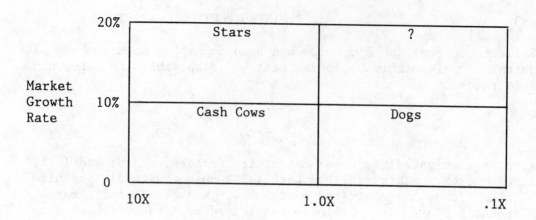

Relative Market Share

$$\text{Relative Market Share} = \frac{\text{Our Company's Share of Market}}{\text{Leading Competitor's Share of Market}}$$

Place the following six circles of Gillette and Bic products in their proper positions within the BCG product portfolio matrix:

Gillette Razors   GR

Gillette Lighters[1]   GL

Gillette Pens   GP

Bic Razors   BR

Bic Lighters   BL

Bic Pens   BP

[1]Does it surprise you to learn that Gillette sold the Cricket line of lighters to Swedish Match in 1984? What reason might Swedish Match have for making the purchase?

Exercise 5-1   MARKET OPPORTUNITY IDENTIFICATION:
                                     EXTERNAL GROWTH STRATEGIES

External growth strategies, in contrast to intensive growth strategies, are growth strategies directed externally to, or outside of, the existing firm. Four major external growth strategies are 1) backward integration, 2) forward integration, 3) horizontal integration, and 4) diversification. Backward integration is a firm's seeking ownership or control of its supply systems. Two common examples are when a retailer sets up its own manufacturing facilities and when a manufacturer buys up a firm producing a major raw material used by the manufacturer. Forward integration is a firm's seeking ownership or control of its distribution systems. Two examples are a manufacturer that sets up its own retail outlets and a wholesaler that sets up its own retail outlets. Horizontal integration is a firm's seeking ownership or control of some competitors. Two examples are when a manufacturer buys out a manufacturing competitor, and when a retailer buys out a retailing competitor. Diversification is an external growth strategy whereby a firm expands outside of its present marketing system.

Instructions: Analyze each of the following statements and indicate which growth strategy is primarily involved.

	Backward Integration	Forward Integration	Horizontal Integration	Diversification
1. The 7-11 Convenience Stores own Oak Farms, which supplies milk and ice cream to the 7-11 stores throughout the United States.	( )	( )	( )	( )
2. G. D. Searles & Co. operates a retail division consisting of over 300 Vision Center Stores. The division recently purchased a number of laboratories that grind lenses and assemble eyeglasses.	( )	( )	( )	( )
3. Household Finance Corporation, the nation's largest consumer finance company, acquired both TG&Y and Ben Franklin variety stores.	( )	( )	( )	( )
4. The Neely Corporation is an East Coast paper manufacturer. It merged with the Hudson Company, another paper manufacturer that produces corrugated fiber boxes.	( )	( )	( )	( )

© 1986 by Prentice-Hall, A Division of Simon & Schuster, Inc.
Englewood Cliffs, N.J. 07632. All rights reserved.
Printed in the United States of America.

	Backward Integration	Forward Integration	Horizontal Integration	Diversification
5. D. H. Baldwin Company manufactures quality pianos and other musical instruments. Baldwin has expanded by buying a number of commercial banks.	( )	( )	( )	( )
6. Nabisco and Standard Brands agreed to merge. Both are food manufacturers, with Nabisco best known for cookies and crackers. Standard Brands produces gelatin, yeast, coffee, and candy bars.	( )	( )	( )	( )
7. Midland Bank, a large commercial bank in Great Britain, merged with Crocker Bank. Crocker is a commercial bank in the United States.	( )	( )	( )	( )
8. Xerox, manufacturer of copying equipment and supplies, dominated its market in its early years but recently it has faced increased competition. In 1981, Xerox opened retail outlets to obtain increased penetration of the low-volume output market.	( )	( )	( )	( )
9. Malone and Hyde, a large Tennessee-based food wholesaler, purchased Piggly Wiggly Corporation in 1982. Piggly Wiggly has approximately 900 retail grocery stores in 21 states.	( )	( )	( )	( )
10. Occidental Petroleum bought Iowa Beef. Occidental is an oil company that has grown greatly in the last 15 years. Iowa Beef pioneered the concept of cutting and prepackaging beef resulting in lower costs at the retail level through reduction in the number of butchers required there.	( )	( )	( )	( )
11. The Canadian Tire Corp., a wholesaler of auto accessories, bought the 81-store White Stores, Inc., in the U.S. in 1982 and tried to apply Canadian product lines to it. In 1984, the White chain had a loss of $55.1 million.	( )	( )	( )	( )

Exercise 5-2

MARKET OPPORTUNITY IDENTIFICATION:
EXTERNAL GROWTH STRATEGIES

External growth strategies, in contrast to intensive growth strategies, are growth strategies directed externally to, or outside of, the existing firm. Four major external growth strategies are 1) backward integration, 2) forward integration, 3) horizontal integration, and 4) diversification. Backward integration is a firm's seeking ownership or control of its supply systems. Two common examples are when a retailer sets up its own manufacturing facilities and when a manufacturer buys up a firm producing a major raw material used by the manufacturer. Forward integration is a firm's seeking ownership or control of its distribution systems. Two examples are a manufacturer that sets up its own retail outlets and a wholesaler that sets up its own retail outlets. Horizontal integration is a firm's seeking ownership or control of some competitors. Two examples are when a manufacturer buys out a manufacturing competitor, and when a retailer buys out a retailing competitor. Diversification is an external growth strategy whereby a firm expands outside of its present marketing system.

Instructions: Analyze each of the following statements and indicate which growth strategy is primarily involved.

	Backward Integration	Forward Integration	Horizontal Integration	Diversification
1. Lone Star Industries, Inc., a leading cement manufacturer, paid Gulf & Western Industries $245 million in cash, stocks, and notes for Marquette Co., another cement maker, returning Lone Star to the number one spot in the North American cement business.	( )	( )	( )	( )
2. Coca Cola Bottling Company of New York is the nation's largest wholesale bottler. It was purchased in 1981 by the worldwide Coca-Cola Company.	( )	( )	( )	( )
3. Batus, the U.S. operating group for the London based B.A.T. Industries, which now owns three large department store chains (Saks Fifth Avenue--32 stores; Gimbels Brothers-- 32 stores; and Marshall Fields & Co.--93 stores) bought Brown & Williamson Tobacco Corp.	( )	( )	( )	( )

© 1986 by Prentice-Hall, A Division of Simon & Schuster, Inc.
Englewood Cliffs, N.J. 07632. All rights reserved.
Printed in the United States of America.

	Backward Integration	Forward Integration	Horizontal Integration	Diversification
4. Pillsbury Company, which manufactures flour and a variety of food products, has purchased Steak and Ale, a chain of restaurants specializing in steaks.	( )	( )	( )	( )
5. Sears Roebuck has bought substantial shares of Kellwood, a manufacturer of durable goods. Kellwood sells a sizable number of products to Sears that are sold under Sears' private label.	( )	( )	( )	( )
6. Stroh's Brewery, located in Detroit, bought out Schlitz Brewery in 1982.	( )	( )	( )	( )
7. Holiday Inns, a chain of motels and hotels, bought a carpet mill. This mill will supply all of the carpet needs of new Holiday Inns.	( )	( )	( )	( )
8. IC Industries, owner of Illinois Gulf Railroad, acquired Midas Mufflers in 1972.	( )	( )	( )	( )
9. Super Valu, the largest food wholesaler in the U.S., has contracted with almost 2000 retail food stores to supply these stores with both food and nonfood products.	( )	( )	( )	( )
10. Humana, Inc., is a profit-making hospital chain. In 1978, Humana acquired American Medicorp, which owned 40 hospitals.	( )	( )	( )	( )
11. Brock Hotel Corp. acquired 51 Chuck E. Cheese Pizza Time Theatre restaurants and 106 franchises from Pizza Time when Pizza Time went bankrupt in 1984.	( )	( )	( )	( )
12. In 1985, Sears Roebuck purchased the Hurley State Bank in South Dakota from which Sears plans to expand distribution of its new Discover credit card to rival American Express, Visa, and MasterCard.	( )	( )	( )	( )

Exercise 5-3

MARKET OPPORTUNITY IDENTIFICATION:
EXTERNAL GROWTH STRATEGIES

External growth strategies, in contrast to intensive growth strategies, are growth strategies directed externally to, or outside of, the existing firm. Four major external growth strategies are 1) backward integration, 2) forward integration, 3) horizontal integration, and 4) diversification. Backward integration is a firm's seeking ownership or control of its supply systems. Two common examples are when a retailer sets up its own manufacturing facilities and when a manufacturer buys up a firm producing a major raw material used by the manufacturer. Forward integration is a firm's seeking ownership or control of its distribution systems. Two examples are a manufacturer that sets up its own retail outlets and a wholesaler that sets up its own retail outlets. Horizontal integration is a firm's seeking ownership or control of some competitors. Two examples are when a manufacturer buys out a manufacturing competitor, and when a retailer buys out a retailing competitor. Diversification is an external growth strategy whereby a firm expands outside of its present marketing system.

Instructions: Analyze each of the following statements and indicate which growth strategy is primarily involved.

	Backward Integration	Forward Integration	Horizontal Integration	Diversification
1. Federated Department Stores bought Rich's Department Store chain. Federated has such stores as Bloomingdale's in New York, Foley's in Houston, and Bullock's in Los Angeles. Rich's is the leading department store chain in Atlanta.	( )	( )	( )	( )
2. In 1982, Norfolk and Western Railroad and Southern Railroad merged to create Norfolk Southern Corporation.	( )	( )	( )	( )
3. General Dynamics Corporation manufactures large defense systems for the Army, Navy, and Air Force. It purchased Chrysler Defense Inc., which manufactures tanks for the Army.	( )	( )	( )	( )
4. Safeway supermarkets have built their own bakeries in many parts of the country. These bakeries supply bread and bakery products	( )	( )	( )	( )

© 1986 by Prentice-Hall, A Division of Simon & Schuster, Inc. Englewood Cliffs, N.J. 07632. All rights reserved. Printed in the United States of America.

	Backward Integration	Forward Integration	Horizontal Integration	Diversification

to the Safeway stores.

5. Coca-Cola Co., producer of soft drinks, citrus fruit drinks, and food products, paid $760 million for Columbia Pictures, a motion picture production company.   ( )   ( )   ( )   ( )

6. Time, Inc., bought Eastex Lumber Company. Time publishes such magazines as Time, Sports Illustrated, and People. Eastex Lumber produces high-quality printing stock.   ( )   ( )   ( )   ( )

7. International Telephone and Telegraph (ITT) purchased the Sheraton hotel chain.   ( )   ( )   ( )   ( )

8. Sherwin-Williams, an established paint manufacturer, opened a group of new retail paint stores.   ( )   ( )   ( )   ( )

9. Prudential Life Insurance Co. has acquired Bache, a leading stock brokerage firm.   ( )   ( )   ( )   ( )

10. McDonald's has been buying back a number of retail stores from its franchisees. McDonald's has pioneered the mass retailing of hamburgers, and is a leader in fast-food franchising.   ( )   ( )   ( )   ( )

11. Diversifoods operates a variety of restaurants and, according to its president, "manages them much like a successful investment portfolio." Diversifoods includes the 887-store Godfather's chain, 377 franchised Burger Kings, 51 Chart House restaurants, and 45 Luther's Bar-B-Que units.   ( )   ( )   ( )   ( )

12. Kmart, the nation's largest chain of discount department stores, believes specialty stores offer future growth. Kmart now owns Furr's Cafeterias, Waldenbooks, Builders Square home improvement stores, and an off-price apparel chain, Designer Depot.   ( )   ( )   ( )   ( )

Exercise 6-1   MARKETING INFORMATION SYSTEM

A marketing information system (MIS) is a structured, interacting complex
of persons, equipment, and procedures designed to generate and analyze an orderly flow of pertinent information for use by marketing managers. The system consists of four subsystems the first of which is the internal reports
system. The internal reports system includes internal records showing such
data as sales, costs, inventories, and accounts receivable and payable. The
second subsystem is the marketing intelligence system. The marketing
intelligence system consists of the daily procedures by which managers gather
information about their industry such as trade papers, conversations with
salespeople and distributors, observations at trade shows, and reading competitors' advertisements. The third subsystem, the marketing research
system, is the formal collection of data about a specific marketing situation, problem, or opportunity facing the manager. The final subsystem, the
analytical marketing system, includes techniques for analyzing the information utilizing quantitative techniques such as statistical procedures and
model building.

> Instruction: Read each of the following statements and
> indicate which subsystem is involved. Select just one
> for each statement.

	Internal Reports	Mktg. Intell.	MR	Analytical
1. When the Gillette Safety Razor Division was considering a proposal to market blank audio recording cassettes, executives read in *Electronics* magazine that the 1970 expected market in business-type dictating machines was estimated to be about 500,000 units.	( )	( )	( )	( )
2. In 1983, in San Antonio, a food broker offered to buy the customer list of a Liberto Specialty Co. subsidiary which distributed nachos to fast-food restaurants throughout the U.S. A loyal employee reported the effort and the broker was arrested after the payoff.	( )	( )	( )	( )
3. For an investigation of liquor consumption patterns for Canada Dry, Grey Advertising agency designed a two-stage study. The first was a group of 20 in-depth interviews and the second a national survey based	( )	( )	( )	( )

© 1986 by Prentice-Hall, A Division of Simon & Schuster, Inc.
Englewood Cliffs, N.J. 07632. All rights reserved.
Printed in the United States of America.

on the material uncovered in the first stage.

4. Prior to deciding on his advertising plans for the marketing of the Model 20 Swinger Land Camera, the general manager determined the gross margin earned on that model was below that earned on other cameras in his line.

( )   ( )   ( )   ( )

5. The president of Hood College in Frederick, Maryland, retained a consulting firm, Stuart Weiner & Associates, to review admissions statistics prior to deciding on a program to attract students.

( )   ( )   ( )   ( )

6. Executives at Fisher Price Toys, Inc., then a subsidiary of Quaker Oats, determined that their highest sales to the trade were in October each year and lowest sales were generally in January or February.

( )   ( )   ( )   ( )

7. Perceptual maps built from multi-dimensional scaling techniques helped explain why the new California attraction, Magic Mountain, had disappointing initial attendance. Consumers viewed it as an imitation of long-established Disneyland.

( )   ( )   ( )   ( )

8. A competitive bidding approach utilizing assigned probabilities and expected awards provided RCA with a procedure that, in seven actual comparisons with normal procedures, resulted in bids that were lower than the competition's by an average of 2%.

( )   ( )   ( )   ( )

9. Goodyear Tire and Rubber Company built a computer-based management information system, connecting company headquarters with all of its more than 1700 service stores, at a cost exceeding $30 million. It provided a daily report on all of the previous day's business.

( )   ( )   ( )   ( )

Exercise 6-2   MARKETING INFORMATION SYSTEM

A marketing information system (MIS) is a structured, interacting complex of persons, equipment, and procedures designed to generate and analyze an orderly flow of pertinent information for use by marketing managers. The system consists of four subsystems, the first of which is the internal reports system. The <u>internal reports system</u> includes internal records showing such data as sales, costs, inventories, and accounts receivable and payable. The second subsystem is the marketing intelligence system. The <u>marketing intelligence system</u> consists of the daily procedures by which managers gather information about their industry such as trade papers, conversations with salespeople and distributors, observations at trade shows, and reading competitors' advertisements. The third subsystem, the <u>marketing research system</u>, is the formal collection of data about a specific marketing situation, problem, or opportunity facing the manager. The final subsystem, the <u>analytical marketing system</u>, includes techniques for analyzing the information utilizing quantitative techniques such as statistical procedures and model building.

Instruction: Read each of the following statements and indicate which subsystem is involved. Select just one for each statement.

	Internal Reports	Mktg. Intell.	MR	Analytical
1. In trying to decide whether to use a general-health promotion, an apple use theme, or no promotion, the Washington State Apple Commission utilized replicated Latin square sequences of treatments. The apple theme was most effective, suggesting that specific uses were more valuable than a general theme.	( )	( )	( )	(✓)
2. In preparing plans for next year, the brand manager for TRAC II, a major shaving product for the Gillette Company, reviewed his firm's sales and contributions to profits by product lines. These figures were a part of the Gillette Annual Report published for investors.	(✓)	( )	( )	( )
3. Prior to adding Maxim, a freeze-dried instant coffee, to its line, General Foods first determined total sales of coffee by obtaining trade association estimates, then reduced this figure by applying management's estimates of	( )	(✓)	( )	( )

© 1986 by Prentice-Hall, A Division of Simon & Schuster, Inc.
Englewood Cliffs, N.J. 07632. All rights reserved.
Printed in the United States of America.

	Internal Reports	Mktg. Intell.	MR	Analytical

the proportion of coffee consumed at home, the proportion of nondecaffeinated coffee, and the instant portion. They then estimated what portion of that figure they could obtain.

4. Having arrived at a physical volume figure in #3 above, executives at General Foods directed that an investigation of the costs of producing and selling that volume be made to determine if a profitable opportunity existed.

( )	(✗)	(✗)	( )

5. Executives at Redbook magazine frequently engage in studies of their female readership designed to provide the marketing staff with information about purchasing habits of readers. These data are then made available to prospective advertisers.

6. Knowing that English steel was thought to be of lower quality than the continental version, an English ironmaster posed as a wandering minstrel and entertained steelworkers at inns all over Europe. He learned their procedures and eventually became Lord Foley, a successful steel producer.

( )	(✓)	(✓)	( )

7. General Food's DreamWhip, a nondairy dry mix that could be blended with milk and whipped into a topping achieved a 50% market share after its introduction. When the firm later introduced the already prepared Cool-Whip product, sales of Dream Whip declined sharply.

( )	( )	( )	( )

8. When Heinz Adam, Federal Express's director of marketing requested his cost accounting department to study the variable costs on each of the three products in Federal's line, they determined that variable costs for the relatively minor product Courier Pak was less than half the cost of each of the other two.

( )	( )	( )	( )

NAME _____

Exercise 6-3   MARKETING INFORMATION SYSTEM

A marketing information system (MIS) is a structured, interacting complex of persons, equipment, and procedures designed to generate and analyze an orderly flow of pertinent information for use by marketing managers. The system consists of four subsystems the first of which is the internal reports system. The <u>internal reports system</u> includes internal records showing such data as sales, costs, inventories, and accounts receivable and payable. The second subsystem is the marketing intelligence system. The <u>marketing intelligence system</u> consists of the daily procedures by which managers gather information about their industry such as trade papers, conversations with salespeople and distributors, observations at trade shows, and reading competitors' advertisements. The third subsystem, the <u>marketing research system</u>, is the formal collection of data about a specific marketing situation, problem, or opportunity facing the manager. The final subsystem, the <u>analytical marketing system</u>, includes techniques for analyzing the information utilizing quantitative techniques such as statistical procedures and model building.

Instructions: Read each of the following statements and indicate which subsystem is involved. Select just one for each statement.

	Internal Reports	Mktg. Intell.	MR	Analytical
1. In 1982, IBM filed a civil suit against Hitachi for stealing confidential information. The suit was settled out of court with Hitachi giving IBM the option to inspect the Japanese firm's new products for five years.	( )	( )	( )	( )
2. In less than four weeks of operation, the number of calls to the 911 emergency telephone number in New York City rose from 12,000 daily under the old 440-1234 number to 18,000 for 911.	( )	( )	( )	( )
3. Detailed study of the 18,000 telephone calls to the 911 number in New York revealed that only 7,000 were real emergencies requiring police.	( )	( )	( )	( )
4. KCTS, the major public television station in Seattle, asked viewers to react to a representative sampling of programs that	( )	( )	( )	( )

© 1986 by Prentice-Hall, A Division of Simon & Schuster, Inc.
Englewood Cliffs, N.J. 07632. All rights reserved.
Printed in the United States of America.

	Internal Reports	Mktg. Intell.	MR	Analytical

KCTS was considering purchasing for the next season . Ballots were printed in the two major newspapers. Over 4,500 were returned within two weeks.

5. When executives at Levi Strauss studied an index of their average wholesale and suggested retail markups for a recent six-year period, they discovered that retail margins had not kept pace with inflation.   ( )   ( )   ( )   ( )

6. Faced with pending federal regulations requiring some sort of passive restraints to be installed on new cars (air bags or automatic seat belts) the manager of GM's Corporate Product Planning Group decided to conduct 25 clinics across the U.S. Existing GM car owners would be exposed to each type of restraint to determine their reactions and preferences.   ( )   ( )   ( )   ( )

7. Executives at Schenley are able to retrieve, within seconds, inventory and sales figures on each of over 400 distributors and compare them to planned performance.   ( )   ( )   ( )   ( )

8. In 1973, the National Association of Food Chains developed COSMOS to calculate a direct product profit for each item in a grocery store. COSMOS stands for Computer Optimization and Simulation Modeling for Operating Supermarkets and costs approximately $50,000 to install.   ( )   ( )   ( )   ( )

9. The Wall Street Journal publishes a column "Abreast of the Market" which highlights noteworthy changes in daily stock prices and summarizes reasons for those changes such as news of a good first quarter earnings report or an expected merger.   ( )   ( )   ( )   ( )

PART THREE

Analyzing Market Opportunities

An awareness of the influence of the environment is critical to decision makers. Marketing success depends on adjusting the controllable elements of the marketing mix to the trends in the uncontrollable environment. An introductory exercise challenges the student to identify the appropriate force affecting a variety of firms. This initial exercise is followed by two that concentrate on one industry each. Exercise 7-2 features forces affecting the insurance industry, and Exercise 7-3 deals with the direct selling, door-to-door, industry.

The second set of exercises concentrates on the importance of managers understanding what occurs as a buyer becomes aware of a need, collects information, evaluates choices and moves through the buyer decision process. The student is eased into learning that the actual purchase is part of a behavioral process. This is done by taking the student through three incident process technique-type exercises that reflect purchase situations that are common in everyday life. Having related the buyer decision process to his or her own situation, the normally unfamiliar world of industrial or organizational buying becomes less mysterious and easier to comprehend. In the third set of exercises, the student is asked to differentiate among straight rebuys, modified rebuys, and new tasks. Such concepts as the amount of new information and the role and level of decision participants are studied.

© 1986 by Prentice-Hall, A Division of Simon & Schuster, Inc.
Englewood Cliffs, N.J. 07632. All rights reserved.
Printed in the United States of America.

Exercise 7-1   ENVIRONMENTAL FORCES

Environmental forces or trends are external and uncontrolled by the firm, so managers must adjust their marketing strategies relative to these externalities. These forces may represent opportunities or threats to the company. Six major forces that represent "uncontrollables" are 1) demographic, 2) economic, 3) natural, 4) technological, 5) political, and 6) cultural. Demographic forces include changing population statistics, including age, geographic shifts, and amount of education. Economic forces include competition, trends in real income, debt and changing consumer buying habits reflecting income changes. Natural forces involves natural shortages, energy costs, and increased pollution. Technological forces include new patents, new technology and R&D efforts. Political forces include existing and potential laws at the federal, state and local level as well as the actions of significant public interest groups. Cultural forces include changing cultural values and social trends.

Instructions: Read each of the following statements and indicate which force is primarily involved. Select just one category for each statement.

	D	E	N	T	P	C
1. Sales of Masonite Corporation's hardboard used in home construction were drastically reduced when high interest rates helped push down housing starts.	( )	( )	( )	( )	( )	( )
2. The 256-RAM computer chip was a scientific breakthrough for computer manufacturers.	( )	( )	( )	( )	( )	( )
3. U.S. Steel has installed over 100 million dollars worth of pollution equipment in order to comply with Environmental Protection Agency (EPA) guidelines.	( )	( )	( )	( )	( )	( )
4. Many small businesses became financially vulnerable in 1982 due to the recession and high rates of interest. Business bankruptcies rose to a record high.	( )	( )	( )	( )	( )	( )
5. With an increased interest in better physical fitness shown by both men and women, there has been a large growth of health spas and other exercising facilities.	( )	( )	( )	( )	( )	( )

© 1986 by Prentice-Hall, A Division of Simon & Schuster, Inc.
Englewood Cliffs, N.J. 07632. All rights reserved.
Printed in the United States of America.

6. New laser-based systems that store
    TV images and sounds on records were
    patented in the early 1980s. The
    video market is expected to rapidly
    expand using this new system.

    ( ) ( ) ( ) ( ) ( ) ( )

7. Curtis Mathis was forced to change
    its advertising message from "the
    24-month full warranty" to "the
    24-month limited warranty" because
    of the Moss-Magnusen Warranty Act.

    ( ) ( ) ( ) ( ) ( ) ( )

8. Taking advantage of the increase in
    the number of working women, Evan-
    Picone has developed a line of
    women's suits for businesswomen.

    ( ) ( ) ( ) ( ) ( ) ( )

9. The number of babies born in the
    Manhattan area of New York City in
    1980 was half the number born in
    1950. Manhattan's population per
    household, 1.96, is the second
    lowest in the nation.

    ( ) ( ) ( ) ( ) ( ) ( )

10. The 55-64 age group is the fastest
    growing in the nation and has an
    estimated 20% of all discretionary
    income.

    ( ) ( ) ( ) ( ) ( ) ( )

11. Because households consisting of
    individuals who have attended
    college spend less money on to-
    bacco, cigarette manufacturers are
    concerned over youngsters' plans
    for college.

    ( ) ( ) ( ) ( ) ( ) ( )

12. In an effort to reducing the pol-
    luting effects of graffiti, the
    City Council of New York prohibited
    in 1985 sales of spray paint and
    broad-tipped markers to people
    under 18 years of age.

    ( ) ( ) ( ) ( ) ( ) ( )

13. Commercial development of the na-
    tion's beaches has been reduced be-
    cause of increasing evidence that
    waves are causing the shorelines
    to recede.

    ( ) ( ) ( ) ( ) ( ) ( )

14. In a Swanson frozen TV-dinner ad, a
    bachelor pretends to have cooked din-
    ner. He impresses his date but finds
    himself helpless when she asks
    for seconds.

    ( ) ( ) ( ) ( ) ( ) ( )

Exercise 7-2   ENVIRONMENTAL FORCES

Environmental forces or trends are external and uncontrolled by the firm, so managers must adjust their marketing strategies relative to these externalities. These forces may represent opportunities or threats to the company. Six major forces that represent "uncontrollables" are 1) demographic, 2) economic, 3) natural, 4) technological, 5) political, and 6) cultural. Demographic forces include changing population statistics, including age, geographic shifts, and amount of education. Economic forces include competition, trends in real income, debt and changing consumer buying habits reflecting income changes. Natural forces involve natural shortages, energy costs, and increased pollution. Technological forces include new patents, new technology and R&D efforts. Political forces include existing and potential laws at the federal, state and local level as well as the actions of significant public interest groups. Cultural forces include changing cultural values and social trends.

Instructions: Read each of the following statements and indicate which force is primarily involved. Select just one category for each statement.

	D	E	N	T	P	C
1. With the development of new medical and drug inventions and patents, the anticipated payments on life insurance policies have been reduced.	( )	( )	( )	( )	( )	( )
2. The increase in the number of competitors offering variable life insurance policies has caused a decline in Metropolitan's life insurance sales.	( )	( )	( )	( )	( )	( )
3. Metropolitan must employ a great number of lawyers to work with state regulatory agencies that regulate the insurance industry.	( )	( )	( )	( )	( )	( )
4. The sale of whole-life insurance policies with their modest investment returns has been adversely affected by the high rate of returns from competing investments.	( )	( )	( )	( )	( )	( )
5. The Federal Trade Commission has investigated a number of insurance firms accused of false and misleading advertising.	( )	( )	( )	( )	( )	( )

© 1986 by Prentice-Hall, A Division of Simon & Schuster, Inc.
Englewood Cliffs, N.J. 07632. All rights reserved.
Printed in the United States of America.

6. Because single people buy less life insurance than married couples, the trend toward later and fewer marriages is adversely affecting the sales of life insurance.

   ( ) ( ) ( ) ( ) ( ) ( )

7. As the percentage of women working continues to increase, this growing market has become attractive to insurance companies.

   ( ) ( ) ( ) ( ) ( ) ( )

8. With the technical improvements in computer services, Metropolitan now gives more timely service at a lower cost to its millions of policyholders.

   ( ) ( ) ( ) ( ) ( ) ( )

9. A number of insurance firms have notified local agents in states bordering the Gulf of Mexico to stop writing hurricane policies whenever a hurricane-force storm has entered the Caribbean Sea.

   ( ) ( ) ( ) ( ) ( ) ( )

10. Because of high costs involving car insurance for teenage males, Metropolitan has contributed to the development of new driver training films for use in high schools.

   ( ) ( ) ( ) ( ) ( ) ( )

11. Because of the increasing number of young affluent women buying option-loaded imported cars, Metropolitan has found this segment to be important in selling car insurance.

   ( ) ( ) ( ) ( ) ( ) ( )

12. The number of families with children dropped 40% between 1970 and 1980 while the number of couples with no children climbed 23%. These changes resulted in some prospective insurance buyers reducing their planned purchases.

   ( ) ( ) ( ) ( ) ( ) ( )

Exercise 7-3   ENVIRONMENTAL FORCES

Environmental forces or trends are external and uncontrolled by the firm, so managers must adjust their marketing strategies relative to these externalities. These forces may represent opportunities or threats to the company. Six major forces that represent "uncontrollables" are 1) demographic, 2) economic, 3) natural, 4) technological, 5) political, and 6) cultural. <u>Demographic forces</u> include changing population statistics, including age, geographic shifts, and amount of education. <u>Economic forces</u> include competition, trends in real income, debt and changing consumer buying habits reflecting income changes. <u>Natural forces</u> involves natural shortages, energy costs, and increased pollution. <u>Technological forces</u> include new patents, new technology and R&D efforts. <u>Political forces</u> include existing and potential laws at the federal, state and local level as well as the actions of significant public interest groups. <u>Cultural forces</u> include changing cultural values and social trends.

      Instructions: Read each of the following statements and indicate which force is primarily involved. Select just one category for each statement.

	<u>D</u>	<u>E</u>	<u>N</u>	<u>T</u>	<u>P</u>	<u>C</u>
1. "Cooling-off" laws, allowing a buyer to cancel a purchase contract signed in the home with door-to-door salespeople, are currently in force in approximately forty states.	( )	( )	( )	( )	( )	( )
2. With the technical development of interactive cable TV through which viewers can purchase items displayed on TV, door-to-door selling may be adversely affected.	( )	( )	( )	( )	( )	( )
3. Door-to-door selling flourished in the post-World War II era of suburban growth when most households in the suburbs contained a women who was home during the day.	( )	( )	( )	( )	( )	( )
4. The major competition to Avon, Mary Kay Cosmetics, has experienced rapid growth in the last few years. Mary Kay Cosmetics' sales in 1981 were $235 million, approximately 50% greater than for 1980.	( )	( )	( )	( )	( )	( )
5. Because of increased concern about and awareness of crime, many individuals who are at home alone are	( )	( )	( )	( )	( )	( )

© 1986 by Prentice-Hall, A Division of Simon & Schuster, Inc.
Englewood Cliffs, N.J. 07632. All rights reserved.
Printed in the United States of America.

reluctant to admit salespeople who
are strangers.

6. In 1981, the Avon chairman stated   ( ) ( ) ( ) ( ) ( ) ( )
   that the performance of Avon prod-
   ucts for the year 1981 was satis-
   factory considering the general
   slowdown of the U.S. economy.

7. Green River-type ordinances are   ( ) ( ) ( ) ( ) ( ) ( )
   laws enacted at the local com-
   munity level. These laws restrict
   salespeople from door-to-door
   solicitation and selling.

8. Dermatology scientists have dis-   ( ) ( ) ( ) ( ) ( ) ( )
   covered that ground apricot pits
   used in a cosmetic facial rub effectively remove dead skin cells.
   Avon has added an apricot product
   to its beauty line.

9. Internal studies by Avon executives ( ) ( ) ( ) ( ) ( ) ( )
   have revealed that their sales-
   people have a tendency to sell
   mainly to their peers.

10. Avon executives are concerned that ( ) ( ) ( ) ( ) ( ) ( )
    their method of distribution may
    not permit them to reach the in-
    creasingly large number of single,
    separated, widowed or divorced
    individuals who must work during
    the day.

11. Should Congress change its current ( ) ( ) ( ) ( ) ( ) ( )
    regulations permitting firms to
    engage in direct selling to view
    its salespeople as independent
    contractors, those companies would
    incur greatly increased costs be-
    cause of requirements of with-
    holding taxes and providing fringe
    benefits that are now not re-
    quired.

12. Hasbro Bradley Inc., manufacturer   ( ) ( ) ( ) ( ) ( ) ( )
    of toys, tried to diversify. Its
    Galloping Gourmet cookware venture
    failed when termites ate the wooden
    salad bowls stacked in a warehouse.

Exercise 8-1   BUYER DECISION PROCESS

The actual purchase is part of a behavioral process that the buyer frequently passes through. This process starts well before the decision to buy and has implications that last beyond the act of purchase. The five stages of the process are 1) problem recognition, 2) information search, 3) evaluation of alternatives, 4) purchase decision, and 5) postpurchase behavior. In the first stage, problem recognition, the buyer becomes aware either internally or externally of a problem or a need for a product or service. If the buyer is uncertain how to solve the problem, an information search commences where the buyer becomes more receptive to advertisements about the item, or discusses with others the satisfaction they have had from competing brands or suppliers. In the third stage, evaluation of alternatives, relevant product or service attributes are weighted and a decision procedure applied. The purchase decision is next in the process and is influenced by one's sensitivity to attitudes of other and unanticipated situational factors that may have arisen such as loss of income or illness. Significantly, the process does not end with the purchase. The final stage involves postpurchase behavior where the buyer compares expected satisfactions from the purchase with perceived performance.

Instructions: Read each of the following statements and indicate which stage is involved. Select just one for each statement.

	PR	IS	EA	PD	PB
1. You join a health fitness club for $200 down and $50 a month for two years under a special promotional offer good only if you join this month.	( )	( )	( )	( )	( )
2. After gaining 15 pounds within the last six months, you find that your friends are kidding you about your eating habits and hide snack foods whenever you appear.	( )	( )	( )	( )	( )
3. At the neighborhood convenience store, you see only one brand of milk and the date stamp on it indicates it should have been sold prior to yesterday.	( )	( )	( )	( )	( )
4. After six months as a member, you are disappointed in the health fitness club because the weight room is always full when	( )	( )	( )	( )	( )

© 1986 by Prentice-Hall, A Division of Simon & Schuster, Inc.
Englewood Cliffs, N.J. 07632. All rights reserved.
Printed in the United States of America.

	PR	IS	EA	PD	PB

you want to use it.

5. You are annoyed over your having to drive to a supermarket to purchase milk, but you do so and while there, decide to buy two gallons of Carnation milk instead of your usual half-gallon size.

( )   ( )   ( )   ( )   ( )

6. Having decided on a diet of no soft drinks, you are annoyed to hear a TV newscast that the beverage you have been drinking has been condemned by health authorities for causing baldness.

( )   ( )   ( )   ( )   ( )

7. The clerk at the convenience store says that he expects a shipment of milk soon because he just saw a Carnation milk truck making a delivery at a nearby supermarket. You consider driving to that supermarket.

( )   ( )   ( )   ( )   ( )

8. Your spouse, upon finding two bottles of Carnation milk in the refrigerator, complains that she prefers another brand because of its taste.

( )   ( )   ( )   ( )   ( )

9. You visit two commercial health clubs and the local YMCA to get information about health facilities and rates. You hope you will have the opportunity to determine how satisfied their customers are.

( )   ( )   ( )   ( )   ( )

10. After a hard workout at the college gym, you realize that when you signed your contract at the private fitness club you had overlooked the alternative of your utilizing the college's health facilities at a very low cost. As you shower, you notice that the water not only is not hot but that the shower room at your private club is dirty.

( )   ( )   ( )   ( )   ( )

Exercise 8-2   BUYER DECISION PROCESS

    The actual purchase is part of a behavioral process that the buyer frequently passes through. This process starts well before the decision to buy and has implications that last beyond the act of purchase. The five stages of the process are 1) problem recognition, 2) information search, 3) evaluation of alternatives, 4) purchase decision, and 5) postpurchase behavior. In the first stage, <u>problem recognition</u>, the buyer becomes aware either internally or externally of a problem or a need for a product or service. If the buyer is uncertain how to solve the problem, an <u>information search</u> commences where the buyer becomes more receptive to advertisements about the item, or discusses with others the satisfaction they have had from competing brands or suppliers. In the third stage, <u>evaluation of alternatives</u>, relevant product or service attributes are weighted and a decision procedure applied. The <u>purchase decision</u> is next in the process and is influenced by one's sensitivity to attitudes of other and unanticipated situational factors that may have arisen such as loss of income or illness. Significantly, the process does not end with the purchase. The final stage involves <u>postpurchase behavior</u> where the buyer compares expected satisfaction from the purchase with perceived performance.

        Instructions: Read each of the following statements and indicate which stage is involved. Select just one for each statement.

	<u>PR</u>	<u>IS</u>	<u>EA</u>	<u>PD</u>	<u>PB</u>
1. Although you debated whether to wait until the end of the semester to have dental work, Dr. Thompson, a dentist in the small town adjacent to the campus, puts a new crown on your left back molar, which has been hurting you.	( )	( )	( )	( )	( )
2. You stop at a city bookstore to compare the price of your required marketing textbook, Kotler, <u>Principles of Marketing</u>, 1986, with the price at the campus bookstore.	( )	( )	( )	( )	( )
3. After you cancelled a third date because of a toothache, your date suggests you see Dr. Thompson, a new dentist in town.	( )	( )	( )	( )	( )

© 1986 by Prentice-Hall, A Division of Simon & Schuster, Inc.
Englewood Cliffs, N.J. 07632. All rights reserved.
Printed in the United States of America.

	PR	IS	EA	PD	PB

4. The syllabus distributed by Professor Jones for the Principles of Marketing course indicated that Kotler, _Principles of Marketing_, 1986, was the required textbook for the course. ( ) ( ) ( ) ( ) ( )

5. When you bit down on a piece of candy at lunch, your left back molar started to ache. ( ) ( ) ( ) ( ) ( )

6. In error, you buy a used copy of Kotler, _Principles of Marketing_, 1983, thinking it will be similar to the 1986 edition required in your Principles of Marketing course. You buy it because it is cheaper than the 1986 book. ( ) ( ) ( ) ( ) ( )

7. You find some questions on your marketing exam that were not covered in your edition of the marketing textbook but you manage to earn a B- by doing very well on the material that was covered. ( ) ( ) ( ) ( ) ( )

8. Being short of funds, you are reluctant to buy the new edition of the required textbook. You attempt to develop a probability estimate of your likelihood of being able to maintain a B average with the older edition. ( ) ( ) ( ) ( ) ( )

9. You initiate a conversation with classmates in an effort to borrow a copy of the new marketing textbook prior to the next exam. ( ) ( ) ( ) ( ) ( )

10. The crown which Dr. Thompson, a local dentist, placed on your back molar is bothering you. You ask the dentist to reexamine it. ( ) ( ) ( ) ( ) ( )

Exercise 8-3   BUYER DECISION PROCESS

The actual purchase is part of a behavior process that the buyer frequently passes through. This process starts well before the decision to buy and has implications that last beyond the act of purchase. The five stages of the process are 1) problem recognition, 2) information search, 3) evaluation of alternatives, 4) purchase decision, and 5) postpurchase behavior. In the first stage, <u>problem recognition</u>, the buyer becomes aware either internally or externally of a problem or a need for a product or service. If the buyer is uncertain how to solve the problem, an <u>information search</u> commences where the buyer becomes more receptive to advertisements about the item, or discusses with others the satisfactions they have had from competing brands or suppliers. In the third stage, <u>evaluation of alternatives</u>, relevant product or service attributes are weighted and a decision procedure applied. The <u>purchase decision</u> is next in the process and is influenced by one's sensitivity to attitudes of other and unanticipated situational factors that may have arisen such as loss of income or illness. Significantly, the process does not end with the purchase. The final stage involves <u>postpurchase behavior</u> where the buyer compares expected satisfactions from the purchase with perceived performance.

Instructions: Read each of the following statements and indicate which stage is involved. Select just one for each statement.

	PR	IS	EA	PD	PB
1. Mr. & Mrs. R. L. Rowe signed a contract with Quality Remodeling Company to add an extra room to their house.	( )	( )	( )	( )	( )
2. Your 1980 convertible automobile has a flat tire five blocks from school and your spare tire is barely usable.	( )	( )	( )	( )	( )
3. You bought a new tire from your retail Goodyear dealer because you saw an advertisement stating the tire was on sale for this week only.	( )	( )	( )	( )	( )
4. Robert and Buffy Rowe are expecting their third child in three months and think they may need to provide more room in their house by remodeling.	( )	( )	( )	( )	( )

© 1986 by Prentice-Hall, A Division of Simon & Schuster, Inc. Englewood Cliffs, N.J. 07632. All rights reserved. Printed in the United States of America.

	PR	IS	EA	PD	PB

5. After looking in the Yellow pages, you telephone three tire dealers and obtain their prices for a new tire for your car.

( ) ( ) ( ) ( ) ( )

6. Two neighbors of the Rowes recommended two home improvement firms for remodeling the Rowe's house, but Robert Rowe is critical of one neighbor's judgment and decides to consider only those remodeling firms that are members of the Better Business Bureau.

( ) ( ) ( ) ( ) ( )

7. The new Goodyear tire on your 1980 convertible develops a slow leak. Because the tire is covered by a warranty, you take it back to the Goodyear dealer to fix it.

( ) ( ) ( ) ( ) ( )

8. Robert and Buffy Rowe are invited to a party in a friend's house where they see a very attractive den that was part of a remodeling job done by one of the firms Robert rejected. Robert is surprised to learn that the job cost about half the Rowe's expected cost.

( ) ( ) ( ) ( ) ( )

9. To assist you in your search for a new tire, you decide to stop by the university library and see which brands rate highly in Consumer Reports magazine. You are primarily interested in tires that perform well in both rain and snow.

( ) ( ) ( ) ( ) ( )

10. Prior to signing a contract, the Rowes receive, in the mail, a circular containing pictures of attractive jobs performed by Quality Remodeling Company together with quotations from satisfied customers.

( ) ( ) ( ) ( ) ( )

Exercise 9-1   INDUSTRIAL BUYER BEHAVIOR

Three basic types of industrial (also called organizational market) buyer behavior are 1) straight rebuy, 2) modified rebuy, and 3) new task. A <u>straight rebuy</u> is a routine purchase, little new information is required, and purchases are generally made from suppliers already on the organization's approved list. The <u>modified rebuy</u> involves new information. Modifications are necessary either because of design changes or because the buying decision makers believe they can obtain improved terms or prices from other suppliers. More information is needed, and several individuals may be involved in the purchase decision. The <u>new task</u> is a very complex decision because the organization is buying something for the first time. There is little past experience to draw on. The greater the risk in the decision, the larger the number of decision participants and the more likely that top management will be involved.

Instructions: Read each of the following statements and indicate which type of industrial buyer behavior is described. Select just one type for each statement.

	Straight Rebuy	Modified Rebuy	New Task
1. Abba Aircraft Company needed to purchase some more electrical wire. The purchasing agent for Abba placed an order with Exact Wire Company, which was on Abba's list of approved suppliers.	( )	( )	( )
2. South Central Bell Telephone Company replaced four-inch-thick cable containing 1,800 copper wires with half-inch fiber optics cable, a completely new concept of sound transmission sold by General Optics.	( )	( )	( )
3. The Thompson Company, manufacturers of grass cloth, placed new orders each spring with its traditional foreign suppliers.	( )	( )	( )
4. Hydraulic pump parts made of die-cast zinc were purchased routinely by the purchasing staff of the West Company until a new supplier proposed that these parts be made of nuclepolyamide plastic with an approximate fifty-percent savings.	( )	( )	( )

© 1986 by Prentice-Hall, A Division of Simon & Schuster, Inc.
Englewood Cliffs, N.J. 07632. All rights reserved.
Printed in the United States of America.

	Straight Rebuy	Modified Rebuy	New Task
5. The Lang Company bought an improved control device from the Sibley Corporation to replace its existing control devices for use in electrical switching problems. The new control device is completely solid-state, and permits "soft starts" by reducing the heavy current flow on an electrical motor.	( )	( )	( )
6. Mr. O'Reily, purchasing manager for the Hudson Turbine Company, was involved in locating suppliers for a new valve assembly required because of a redesign. He sent requests for bids to twelve firms, eight of which had supplied assemblies for previous designs.	( )	( )	( )
7. In 1973, the H. J. Heinz Company's purchases of ketchup bottles amounted to over $15 million annually. Approximately equal amounts were purchased from three major suppliers.	( )	( )	( )
8. The purchasing agent at AGR Corporation needs to purchase a standard component on an assembly drive used in one of AGR's basic products. He has a proposal from a Japanese supplier whose price is 23% below what AGR is paying its major U.S. supplier. The agent is uncertain about the reliability of ocean freight.	( )	( )	( )
9. The Adamson Corporation is considering its first purchase of a company airplane. Although the president of the company has formed a committee to recommend a choice, she expects to make the final decision.	( )	( )	( )

Exercise 9-2   INDUSTRIAL BUYER BEHAVIOR

Three basic types of industrial (also called organizational market) buyer behavior are 1) straight rebuy, 2) modified rebuy, and 3) new task. A straight rebuy is a routine purchase, little new information is required, and purchases are generally made from suppliers already on the organization's approved list. The modified rebuy involves new information. Modifications are necessary either because of design changes or because the buying decision makers believe they can obtain improved terms or prices from other suppliers. More information is needed, and several individuals may be involved in the purchase decision. The new task is a very complex decision because the organization is buying something for the first time. There is little past experience to draw on. The greater the risk in the decision, the larger the number of decision participants and the more likely that top management will be involved.

Instructions: Read each of the following statements and indicate which type of industrial buyer behavior is described. Select just one type for each statement.

	Straight Rebuy	Modified Rebuy	New Task
1. The Blair Manufacturing Corporation has decided to manufacture some new heavy machinery that cannot be made with its existing equipment. The purchasing department worked closely with the engineering design department to identify possible suppliers of the needed production equipment.	( )	( )	( )
2. The Fulbright Supply Company, distributors of chemicals, purchased acetone in equal amounts from three major suppliers in order to maintain good sources of supply and competitive terms.	( )	( )	( )
3. Central States Lighting and Power Company, planning the construction of a new 800-megawatt power plant burning pulverized coal, notified prospective suppliers of the firm's need for bids on furnaces to develop steam for the plant's turbines.	( )	( )	( )
4. Turnham Co., manufacturers of diesel-engine parts, received several large orders for its standard product. The	( )	( )	( )

© 1986 by Prentice-Hall, A Division of Simon & Schuster, Inc. Englewood Cliffs, N.J. 07632. All rights reserved. Printed in the United States of America.

	Straight Rebuy	Modified Rebuy	New Task

purchasing manager ordered additional inventory from his approved list of suppliers.

5. When its regular supplier abruptly increased its prices for component parts, the RLW Company made a search for new suppliers whose prices would be more attractive, yet who would supply according to RLW's required production schedule.   ( )   ( )   ( )

6. When the primary supplier had a disastrous fire that interrupted its delivery schedule, the Mason Corporation decided to change its policies on vendors and sought out new suppliers. Management planned to divide its orders among three, but first had to qualify those firms by inspecting their production facilities.   ( )   ( )   ( )

7. Upon return from a hospital stay, Mr. L. P. Polk, purchasing manager for the West Side Office Supply Company, found that the supplies of standard $8\frac{1}{2}$ x 11 typewriting paper was low. He telephoned a replacement order to his primary supplier.   ( )   ( )   ( )

8. For years, the Diddley Corporation used corrugated packing material for shipping its products. A new supplier, Curmont Plastics, has proposed that the products be shipped in a new, airtight, plastic pro--tective cover. The purchasing department has called a meeting of the vice presidents of production and marketing to review the feasibility of the proposal.   ( )   ( )   ( )

9. Mr. S. L. Gross, purchasing manager for RWL's roller bearing division, met with four of its grinding material suppliers. He wanted a supplier to provide inventory to RWL's plant that would be charged to RWL only when removed from inventory.   ( )   ( )   ( )

Exercise 9-3   INDUSTRIAL BUYER BEHAVIOR

Three basic types of industrial (also called organizational market) buyer behavior are 1) straight rebuy, 2) modified rebuy, and 3) new task. A <u>straight rebuy</u> is a routine purchase, little new information is required, and purchases are generally made from suppliers already on the organization's approved list. The <u>modified rebuy</u> involves new information. Modifications are necessary either because of design changes or because the buying decision makers believe they can obtain improved terms or prices from other suppliers. More information is needed, and several individuals may be involved in the purchase decision. The <u>new task</u> is a very complex decision because the organization is buying something for the first time. There is little past experience to draw on. The greater the risk in the decision, the larger the number of decision participants and the more likely that top management will be involved.

> Instructions: Read each of the following statements and indicate which type of industrial buyer behavior is described. Select just one type for each statement.

	Straight Rebuy	Modified Rebuy	New Task
1. Part number R418 is a metal reproduction of the name of the manufacturer and is attached to each item made by the Wallace Corporation. The style of the logo was determined several years ago and is not expected to change in the near future. The purchasing agent is pleased with the price and delivery arrangements of the existing supplier.	( )	( )	( )
2. In order to reduce costs, Mr. J. M. Wilson, purchasing manager of the Wallace Corporation, requests that the design engineers investigate the use of lower-quality gaskets in the firm's lower-price line of submersible pumps, rather than continue to assemble the same gaskets that were used in the premium-quality line.	( )	( )	( )
3. The Wallace Corporation ships 60 percent of its output in corrugated paper boxes that it purchases from three suppliers. The New Era Company has opened a new plant nearby and offers a very low price if Wallace will concentrate half of its box purchases for the next two	( )	( )	( )

© 1986 by Prentice-Hall, A Division of Simon & Schuster, Inc.
Englewood Cliffs, N.J. 07632. All rights reserved.
Printed in the United States of America.

	Straight Rebuy	Modified Rebuy	New Task

years from New Era. Also, New Era requests a simpler box design.

4. Institutional trash bags, used by the Wallace Corp.'s janitorial force nightly, are supplied by a janitorial supply house in large lots. The existing supplier has a variety of bag sizes.   ( )   ( )   ( )

5. Upon arriving at his office, Mr. Wilson was informed that three of the firm's five new forklift trucks had been stolen the night before. Under considerable pressure from the shipping dock foreman, Mr. Wilson purchased two trucks by phone. He ordered from the firm that had the best bid when the Wallace Corp. had reviewed proposals for forklift trucks last year.   ( )   ( )   ( )

6. The head of Wallace's research department has requested Mr. Wilson's assistance in buying a new electronic microscope for the company laboratory. Wallace is considering entering several new fields.   ( )   ( )   ( )

7. Mr. Wilson has been authorized to arrange for the purchase of a robotics unit for installation in a pilot plant operation. No one at the Wallace Corp. has had much experience in this area.   ( )   ( )   ( )

8. Concerned over what he felt to be rising costs of traditional telephone service, the president of Wallace appointed a high-level task force to study the problem. The task force recommended that Wallace lease new private transmission lines.   ( )   ( )   ( )

9. Mr. Wilson is approached by a German chemical firm that is willing to supply his need for sulphuric acid. The proposed price is 17% below the current U.S. market, but Wallace would have to receive shipments in railroad tank cars rather than by truck. Wilson does not know if the larger quantity is acceptable to his stores department.   ( )   ( )   ( )

PART FOUR

Selecting Target Markets

Marketers match products to markets. Sometimes markets are so large and include such a variety of buyers that marketers find it more profitable to break the market down into particular segments and to design different products for each segment. The four major types of market segmentation appear in the three sets of Exercise 10. The student is faced with twenty-nine examples of profitable segmentation by a variety of marketers ranging from General Motors and Heilman Brewing Company to the television networks that telecast "Dynasty" and "Dallas."

Three alternative target marketing strategies available to marketers are examined in the second group of exercises. The three exercises in total contain thirty-one situations where the student's ability to distinguish among undifferentiated, differentiated, and concentrated strategy is tested. Current examples include Eastern Airline's "moonlight specials" for limited passenger service on its primarily cargo flights and the Ritz-Carlton Hotel's emphasis upon serving the businessperson in New York City.

© 1986 by Prentice-Hall, A Division of Simon & Schuster, Inc.
Englewood Cliffs, N.J. 07632. All rights reserved.
Printed in the United States of America.

Exercise 10-1   MARKET SEGMENTATION

Managers have found it useful to divide the total market into segments or groups of buyers who have similar wants for which an organization might profitably provide a product or service. Although marketing authorities differ on their classifications of segments, most approaches include classification of consumer behavior, as well as of consumer characteristics. Four types of segmentation are 1) geographic segmentation, 2) demographic segmentation, 3) psychographic segmentation and 4) behavioristic segmentation. Geographic segmentation reflects variation in buyer needs or responses based on differences related to regions or locations. Demographic segmentation recognizes the differences affected by such variables as age, sex, nationality, religion, education, family size, income, etc. Psychographic segmentation reflects differences related to attitudes, interests, or opinions that result in differing social class, life styles, and personalities. Behavioristic segmentation divides buyers into different groups based on a) the direct product-related benefits they seek from the offering such as durability or prestige; b) the occasions when they use it, such as a holiday versus everyday use; c) user status such as first time or regular users; d) usage rate; e) buyer readiness stage, which includes degree of awareness of the product; and f) attitude toward the offering such as enthusiastic or indifferent.

Instruction: Read each of the following statements and indicate which type of segmentation is described. Select just one type for each statement.

	Geo-graphic	Demo-graphic	Psycho-graphic	Behav-ioristic
1. The number of families with children dropped 40% between 1970 and 1980, while the number of couples with no children climbed 23%. Many of the latter are two-income households that are transforming old, inner-city neighborhoods of large apartments or run-down homes into fashionable smaller apartments and remodeled townhouses.	( )	( )	( )	( )
2. After establishing a successful store, The Children's Collection, the owners opened Collection II next door to cater to preteens who had formerly shopped at their first store. Items stocked reflect teenage style because "what teenagers wear is the rule for preteens, but in their sizes."	( )	( )	( )	( )
3. Executives at General Motors have	( )	( )	( )	( )

© 1986 by Prentice-Hall, A Division of Simon & Schuster, Inc.
Englewood Cliffs, N.J. 07632. All rights reserved.
Printed in the United States of America.

	Geo-graphic	Demo-graphic	Psycho-graphic	Behav-ioristic

been quoted as saying that the Chevy Citation is aimed at a group that is more concerned with the quality of life than an economically measured standard of living. This group supposedly demands well-equipped cars because "they don't skimp."

		Geo-graphic	Demo-graphic	Psycho-graphic	Behav-ioristic
4.	Heilman Brewing Company, headquartered in LaCrosse, Wisconsin, competes with Budweiser and Miller. It does not distribute nationally. By acquiring small regional breweries, it keeps locally respected labels and designs marketing programs specifically for each region.	( )	( )	( )	( )
5.	Because 70% of its gasoline sales were to repeat customers who paid cash, Atlantic Richfield Co. (Arco) stopped honoring credit cards in 1982 and planned to reduce its price to distributors and dealers by three cents per gallon.	( )	( )	( )	( )
6.	A paint manufacturer believes that his market can be divided into four completely separated segments which he calls Helpless Homemaker, Handy Helper, Craftsman, and Cost-conscious Couples.	( )	( )	( )	( )
7.	According to Pizza Hut, Easterners like plenty of cheese in their pizza, Westerners prefer a variety of ingredients, and Midwesterners like both.	( )	( )	( )	( )
8.	Prime Time is a magazine aimed at the forty-and-over segment with articles in a recent issue devoted to such topics as retirement planning, healthy use of leisure time, avoiding depression, and "Skiing the Way It Used to Be."	( )	( )	( )	( )
9.	Because a large percentage of the customers of the Oakland, California, retail furniture store, Liberty House Mainland, are apartment dwellers, the management emphasizes smaller sofa beds and de-emphasizes carpets and draperies, which generally come with an apartment.	( )	( )	( )	( )

Exercise 10-2   MARKET SEGMENTATION

Managers have found it useful to divide the total market into segments or groups of buyers who have similar wants for which an organization might profitably provide a product or service. Although marketing authorities differ on their classifications of segments, most approaches include classi-fication of consumer behavior, as well as of consumer characteristics. Four types of segmentation are 1) geographic segmentation, 2) demographic segmen-tation, 3) psychographic segmentation and 4) behavioristic segmentation. Geographic segmentation reflects variation in buyer needs or responses based on differences related to regions or locations. Demographic segmentation recognizes the differences affected by such variables as age, sex, nation-ality, religion, education, family size, income, etc. Psychographic segmen-tation reflects differences related to attitudes, interests, or opinions that result in differing social class, life styles, and personalities. Behavioristic segmentation divides buyers into different groups based on a) the direct product-related benefits they seek from the offering, such as durability or prestige; b) the occasions when they use it such as holiday versus everyday use; c) user status such as first time or regular users; d) usage rate; e) buyer readiness stage which includes degree of awareness of the product; and f) attitude toward the offering, such as enthusiastic or indifferent.

Instruction: Read each of the following statements and indicate which type of segmentation is described. Select just one type for each statement.

	Geo-graphic	Demo-graphic	Psycho-graphic	Behav-ioristic
1. The Millionaires Club for Singles was designed to helping "trusting, successful oriented individuals who are financially responsible ... to meet people with whom they share com-mon lifestyles and values." Money itself is not a condition for mem-bership.	( )	( )	( )	( )
2. Seven-Up Company test-marketed Like, a sugar-free, caffeine-free cola in 1982, after observing that the sugarless soft drink segment was growing at an annual 8 percent rate.	( )	( )	( )	( )
3. People who live in the West are more likely to buy a stronger coffee than people in the East.	( )	( )	( )	( )
4. The single-person household has be-come an important market segment.	( )	( )	( )	( )

© 1986 by Prentice-Hall, A Division of Simon & Schuster, Inc.
Englewood Cliffs, N.J. 07632. All rights reserved.
Printed in the United States of America.

	Geo-graphic	Demo-graphic	Psycho-graphic	Behav-ioristic
Individuals who are single, separated, widowed, or divorced buy 26% of all passenger cars but 50% of Ford Mustangs and other specialty cars.	( )	( )	( )	( )
5. The high-powered "muscle cars" of the mid-Sixties disappeared in 1974 when the energy crunch hit the U.S. In 1982 the Ford Motor Company introduced an H.O. (high output) Mercury Capri with "our ultimate engine option," a V-8 for owners desiring high performance cars.	( )	( )	( )	( )
6. Ford Motor Co. has introduced Aerostar, its small van, aimed at being "the most beautiful truck ever built" according to the Ford vice president for sales operations.	( )	( )	( )	( )
7. Two non-Hispanics are successfully operating the seven-store supermarket chain Fiesta Markets, Inc., in the southwest U.S. catering to Hispanics and featuring low-priced staples. Recently, Fiesta added Vietnamese food products.	( )	( )	( )	( )
8. The management of Adolph Coors Brewery has restricted its market to neighboring states that can be serviced by refrigerated delivery trucks.	( )	( )	( )	( )
9. The 315-room Royal American Hotel and Casino in Las Vegas was closed in 1982, not because its hotel occupancy rate was low (it averaged 80%), but because its small rooms and modest decor attracted only small bettors into its gambling rooms.	( )	( )	( )	( )
10. In a significant study in 1968, researcher Russell I. Haley identified an important segment of the toothpaste market to be the worrier segment, which was somewhat hypochondriac. This group disproportionately preferred Crest over other brands.	( )	( )	( )	( )

Name _Joseph Lopez_

Exercise 10-3   MARKET SEGMENTATION

Managers have found it useful to divide the total market into segments or groups of buyers who have similar wants for which an organization might profitably provide a product or service. Although marketing authorities differ on their classifications of segments, most approaches include classification of consumer behavior, as well as of consumer characteristics. Four types of segmentation are 1) geographic segmentation, 2) demographic segmentation, 3) psychographic segmentation and 4) behavioristic segmentation. Geographic segmentation reflects variation in buyer needs or responses based on differences related to regions or locations. Demographic segmentation recognizes the differences affected by such variables as age, sex, nationality, religion, education, family size, income, etc. Psychographic segmentation reflects differences related to attitudes, interests or opinions that result in differing social class, life styles, and personalities. Behavioristic segmentation divides buyers into different groups based on a) the direct product-related benefits they seek from the offering such as durability or prestige; b) the occasions when they use it such as holiday versus everyday use; c) user status such as first time or regular users; d) usage rate; e) buyer readiness stage which includes degree of awareness of the product; and f) attitude toward the offering, such as enthusiastic or indifferent.

Instruction: Read each of the following statements and indicate which type of segmentation is described. Select just one type for each statement.

	Geographic	Demographic	Psychographic	Behavioristic
1. While ABC's "Dynasty" and CBS's "Dallas" prime time TV dramas have about equivalent demographic audiences, the media research firm Information Resource, Inc., believes "Dynasty" has a higher households-using-TV level among heavy grocery buyers.	( )	( )	( )	(✓)
2. The new Ford Motor Co.'s Merkur XR4Ti "has everything standard that the ultimate yuppie wants: high performance, superior acceleration, cornering, braking, and top stereo." Because of limited supplies, the new car was originally restricted to the West Coast.	(✓)	(✓)	(✓)	(✓)
3. The Dunston Corp., manufacturer of industrial products, distributes	( )	( )	( )	( )

© 1986 by Prentice-Hall, A Division of Simon & Schuster, Inc.
Englewood Cliffs, N.J. 07632. All rights reserved.
Printed in the United States of America.

	Geo-graphic	Demo-graphic	Psycho-graphic	Behav-ioristic

through manufacturers' agents in territories of low potential, but distributes through its own sales branch offices in high potential territories.

	Geo-graphic	Demo-graphic	Psycho-graphic	Behav-ioristic
4. Miller Brewing Company made Miller Lite a highly successful product introduction by aiming it not at the low-calorie market but at the heavy beer drinker who wanted a less filling beer so that more beer could be consumed.	( )	( )	( )	( )
5. Residents of Pittsburgh are fifty percent more likely to buy mouth-wash than are residents of Atlanta.	(✓)	( )	( )	( )
6. Discovering that only 20% of card-holders were women, American Express modified its advertising to include TV commercials featuring confident, independent women using credit cards.	( )	( )	( )	( )
7. Borrowers who lack self-confidence are more likely to borrow from con-sumer finance companies than from banks.	( )	( )	(✓)	( )
8. In 1982, Stouffer's, a producer of high-quality, prepared, frozen food entrees, introduced Lean Cuisine, a line of low-calorie full-portion entrees, including beef dishes, sea-food, and pasta. The market de-siring low-calorie foods responded so well that year that Stouffer's could not meet the demand.	( )	( )	( )	( )
9. Goya Foods, Inc., with a line of 700 Hispanic specialty foods, caters to the 14.6 million Hispanic market, which is growing faster than any other minority group.	( )	( )	( )	( )
10. Noting that 70% of Tab drinkers were women, Coca-Cola Co. manage-ment markets Diet Coke to a broader market.	( )	(✓)	( )	( )

Exercise 11-1   TARGET MARKETING STRATEGY

   Most firms consider three broad alternative strategies in targeting
their marketing efforts to opportunities in the marketplace. Undifferentiated marketing strategy treats the market as an aggregate; the firm
designs a marketing program that appeals to the broadest number of buyers.
Differentiated marketing strategy segments the total market into multiple
segments; the firm designs marketing programs for each segment. Concentrated marketing strategy is marketing to one customer segment or a few
segments rather than the total marketplace.

          Instructions: Read each of the following statements
          and indicate which strategy is involved. Select just
          one for each statement.

	Undiffer-entiated Strategy	Differen-tiated Strategy	Concen-trated Strategy
1. Chicago home builder Ralph Smyka offers homes in suburban Naperville that abut a private airstrip. There is room enough on the lots for each owner to have a hanger. Smyka points out that other developments have built homes along waterways for boaters and along fairways for golfers.	( )	( )	( )
2. Although Eastern Airline's primary market is business travelers, the carrier initiated cut-rate, late-night "moonlight specials " on its transcontinental cargo flights through its Houston hub. Passengers, who pay extra for meals and cannot check baggage, can fly cross-country for $98 if they are willing to board one hour before flight time and recognize that delays in Houston may occur.	( )	( )	( )
3. The Short Shop in San Francisco is a men's retail store that sells to short men. In the store, the mirrors are short, the checkout counters are low, and the coat racks are close to the floor.	( )	( )	( )
4. The table salt market is dominated by Morton salt, which sells more table salt than all of its competitors combined. "When it rains, it pours" has	( )	( )	( )

© 1986 by Prentice-Hall, A Division of Simon & Schuster, Inc.
Englewood Cliffs, N.J. 07632. All rights reserved.
Printed in the United States of America.

	Undiffer-entiated Strategy	Differen-tiated Strategy	Concen-trated Strategy

been Morton's slogan in selling the table salt market.

5. Coca Cola is the leading manufacturer of soft drinks in the world. Coke competes for multiple segments of the market with such brands as Coca Cola, Mr. Pibb, Tab, Diet Coke, and Sprite.   ( )   ( )   ( )

6. Southwest Airlines started its business by flying between Dallas, Houston, and San Antonio. By using airports close to the cities, Southwest aimed their service narrowly at the business commuter market.   ( )   ( )   ( )

7. The U.S. Post Office is a government agency that handles large volumes of mail. The Post Office is designed to fill the needs of everybody who needs to mail something.   ( )   ( )   ( )

8. Anheuser-Busch Company, with headquarters in St. Louis, sells more beer in the United States than any of its competitors. Michelob sells to the upper-premium market, Budweiser sells to the premium market, Busch Bavarian sells to the popular-priced market, and Budweiser Light sells to the calorie-conscious market.   ( )   ( )   ( )

9. Fisher-Price is a well-known manufacturer of toys. Rather than produce all types of toys, Fisher-Price has developed pre-school toys for the children's market.   ( )   ( )   ( )

10. General Motors tries to sell everybody a GM product. Cadillac sells to the business market, Chevrolet sells to the working-class market and Oldsmobile sells to the middle class market.   ( )   ( )   ( )

Exercise 11-2   TARGET MARKETING STRATEGY

Most firms consider three broad alternative strategies in targeting their marketing efforts to opportunities in the marketplace. Undifferentiated marketing strategy treats the market as an aggregate; the firm designs a marketing program that appeals to the broadest number of buyers. Differentiated marketing strategy segments the total market into multiple segments; the firm designs marketing programs for each segment. Concentrated marketing strategy is marketing to one customer segment or a few segments rather than the total marketplace.

Instructions: Read each of the following statements and indicate which strategy is involved. Select just one for each statement.

	Undifferentiated Strategy	Differentiated Strategy	Concentrated Strategy
1. To offset the perception that its beers are lighter tasting than competitors, Adolph Coors introduced a Coors Extra Gold brand with 30-second TV spots using macho messages saying, "This is bolder, golder, broad-shouldered beer," and "Beer with a taste you can see."	( )	( )	( )
2. Although the average U.S. male is five feet nine, 25% are five feet seven or under. Detroit's Napoleon's Closet is a men's retail clothing store that sells to small men.	( )	( )	( )
3. TV Guide is a weekly magazine with circulation over twenty million copies per week. Everybody with access to television is a potential customer for TV Guide.	( )	( )	( )
4. Medi-Clinic is a freestanding medical clinic. Medi-Clinic's primary customers are people who don't have a regular family physician.	( )	( )	( )
5. The Children's Museum in Denver is targeted for families with two or more children. In addition to building a new $3.2 million museum, the Children's Museum sponsors numerous travelling exhibits and special promotions.	( )	( )	( )

© 1986 by Prentice-Hall, A Division of Simon & Schuster, Inc. Englewood Cliffs, N.J. 07632. All rights reserved. Printed in the United States of America.

	Undiffer-entiated Strategy	Differen-tiated Strategy	Concen-trated Strategy
6. Bristol-Meyers has introduced three leading products to compete in the analgesic market. Bufferin aspirin is positioned for the simple pain customers, Excedrin aspirin is positioned for the severe pain customers, and Datril is positioned for the nonaspirin customers.	( )	( )	( )
7. PACCAR is a relatively small company in Seattle that produces heavy diesel trucks in competition with General Motors, Ford, International Harvester, and Mack. PACCAR's major brand, Peterbilt, is aimed at the independent trucker, not the large fleet operators.	( )	( )	( )
8. Philip Morris is a large cigarette manufacturer that targets its products to all cigarette smokers, including the female segment, the health (low-tar) segment, and the heavy user segment. Some of Philip Morris brands include Marlboro, Merit, Virginia Slims, and Benson and Hedges.	( )	( )	( )
9. For years the Hershey company made one basic product, Hershey's chocolate. With a good reputation for quality, Hershey's market was for all people.	( )	( )	( )
10. Procter & Gamble products sells to over 50 percent of the total soap market. Different types of soap customers are appealed to by such well-known P&G soap products as Ivory, Zest, and Camay.	( )	( )	( )

NAME *Joseph Ropon*

Exercise 11-3   TARGET MARKETING STRATEGY

Most firms consider three broad alternative strategies in targeting their marketing efforts to opportunities in the marketplace. <u>Undifferentiated marketing strategy</u> treats the market as an aggregate; the firm designs a marketing program that appeals to the broadest number of buyers. <u>Differentiated marketing strategy</u> segments the total market into multiple segments; the firm designs marketing programs for each segment. <u>Concentrated marketing strategy</u> is marketing to one customer segment or a few segments rather than the total marketplace.

Instructions: Read each of the following statements and indicate which strategy is involved. Select just one for each statement.

	Undifferentiated Strategy	Differentiated Strategy	Concentrated Strategy
1. Citytrust Bancorp's Bridgeport bank directs its efforts at small firms--those with $1 million to $25 million in sales--and offers individual services that appeal to officers and owners of such businesses. Earnings have increased an average of 25% a year.	( )	( )	(✓)
2. Concerned that it had developed an image of offering strange-looking cars to older, lower income buyers, American Motors Corp. signed an agreement with French producer Renault and produced Renault Alliance sedans as well as selling the Renault Fuego, a spiffy, small, front-wheel-drive sports car.	( )	( )	( )
3. General Foods is a leading producer of coffee in the United States, and competes across the board, with its major competitors, Folgers and Nestle. Sanka, Maxwell House, and Yuban are three GF brands that sell to different types of coffee drinkers.	(✓)	( )	( )
4. Gerber is a large food processor located in Michigan. While their competitors, such as Swift, Heinz, and Beechnut, produced food products for many types of customers, Gerber focused on the baby market for its products.	( )	( )	(✓)

© 1986 by Prentice-Hall, A Division of Simon & Schuster, Inc.
Englewood Cliffs, N.J. 07632. All rights reserved.
Printed in the United States of America.

	Undifferentiated Strategy	Differentiated Strategy	Concentrated Strategy
5. Lever Brothers has competed with Colgate and Procter & Gamble over the years for the toothpaste business. Lever has sold Pepsodent to the older-consumer market, Close-Up to the teenage market, and Aim to the cavity-sensitive market.	( )	(✓)	( )
6. Sears Roebuck is the largest retailer in the United States in sales. Its home offices are in Chicago. Sears tries to sell to almost everybody.	( )	( )	( )
7. Continental Bakery, maker of Wonder bread, sells its bread product in the United States to virtually every person using bread.	(✓)	( )	( )
8. Richard D. Irwin is a college book publisher. Rather than sell books in all college disciplines, Irwin has developed an extensive line of textbooks in the business and economic disciplines.	( )	( )	(✓)
9. With a 40 percent share of the total cereal market, Kellogg competes in the children segment with Frosted Flakes and in the adult segment with Raisin Bran.	( )	( )	( )
10. The Ritz-Carlton is a New York City hotel where "accommodating executives is not a business but an art." The Ritz-Carlton caters to business executives who want exquisite hotel services.	( )	( )	( )
11. The superintendent of the Chicago Police Force gave serious consideration to the appointment of a director of marketing.	( )	( )	( )

PART FIVE

Developing the Marketing Mix

This giant section contains twenty-one sets of exercises devoted to the "four P's" of the marketing mix. The twenty-one sets include four sets of quantitative case problems.

The section opens with two product line modification case problems requiring quantitative analysis. They concern two concepts: contribution to fixed costs and break-even point. Because some students have difficulty with contribution as a concept, this subject is reviewed again in a number of the quantitative-type case problems dealing with the remaining elements of the marketing mix: pricing, distribution, and promotion. This repeated exposure to contribution in a variety of market mix situations enables the student to learn the usefulness of the concept in analyzing alternative marketing-mix programs so that it becomes an integral part of the student's skills in marketing problem-solving.

Each of the four sets of quantitative problems (a total of sixteen problems) introduces a different section of this part of the manual. The two product line modification problems introduce the product section. There follow five sets of qualitative exercises, including those devoted to the classification of consumer goods, branding, and product life-cycle topics. The five pricing problems of Exercise 18 are followed by three sets of regular exercises on pricing, pricing strategy, and price discounts. Four distribution problems introduce the topics of channel conflict, vertical marketing systems, distribution coverage strategy, and types of wholesalers. The final "P" of the "four "P's" is promotion. Five problems on such topics as advertising budget determination, sales territory analysis and salesforce performance introduce the large topic of promotion. Individual sets of three exercises each are devoted to marketing communications, appropriation determination, push/pull strategies, the personal selling process, and types of sales positions.

© 1986 by Prentice-Hall, A Division of Simon & Schuster, Inc.
Englewood Cliffs, N.J. 07632. All rights reserved.
Printed in the United States of America.

Exercise 12-1   QUANTITATIVE ANALYSIS: PRODUCT-LINE
                                 MODIFICATION--Goldman's Department
                                 Store

Problem

     Goldman's Department Store is a medium sized department store in the
Midwest. Goldman's share of market has been declining and is presently
16%. With profits also declining the last two years, top management com-
missioned a cost accounting study. The profitability of the five major
departments in the store was:

Departments	Sales ($1,000)	Contribution ($1,000)
1	$1,400	$ 100
2	3,200	800
3	800	200
4	3,100	700
5	2,500	700

     Fixed Cost was $2,200,000.

1. Compute sales, contribution, and net profit.

                    Sales _____

              Contribution _____

                Net Profit _____

© 1986 by Prentice-Hall, A Division of Simon & Schuster, Inc.
Englewood Cliffs, N.J. 07632. All rights reserved.
Printed in the United States of America.

Contribution   =   Sales - Variable Costs

Net Profit   =   Contribution - Fixed Costs

$$\text{Break Even Point} = \frac{\text{Fixed Costs}}{\text{Unit Sales Price - Unit Variable Costs}}$$

Fixed Costs: The cost is fixed if it remains constant over a relevant range even when the volume of activity varies.

Variable Costs: The cost is variable if it changes when the volume of activity changes.

2.   Management was considering adding a new major department (#6). Sales in the new department were estimated to be $800,000 with a contribution of $200,000. No changes in fixed costs were anticipated if department #6 replaced department #1. Compute sales, contribution, and net profit if department #1 is eliminated and department #6 is added.

Sales _____

Contribution _____

Net Profit _____

NAME _____

Exercise 12-2

QUANTITATIVE ANALYSIS: PRODUCT-LINE
MODIFICATION--The Thompson Industrial
Company

Problem

The Thompson Industrial Company is an industrial firm located in a
large Midwestern city. The company sells five different product lines in
which the basic raw material is steel and aluminum flat coil plates. At
the present time, Thompson has a 12% share of market, and the total industry
is considered to be in the mature stage of the product's life cycle. The top
two products account for 90% of the contribution to profit. After a cost
accounting study, the current profitability of the product lines was estimated to be:

Product Lines	Sales ($1,000)	Variable Costs ($1,000)	Contribution ($1,000)
A	$ 4,800	$ 3,800	$ 1,000
B	4,000	3,200	800
C	3,800	3,400	400
D	3,900	3,800	100
E	3,500	3,800	(300)
	$20,000	$18,000	$ 2,000

Fixed Cost was $1,500,000.

Net Profit was $500,000.

© 1986 by Prentice-Hall, A Division of Simon & Schuster, Inc.
Englewood Cliffs, N.J. 07632. All rights reserved.
Printed in the United States of America.

<u>Basic Concepts to Apply</u>

$$\text{Contribution} = \text{Sales} - \text{Variable Costs}$$

$$\text{Net Profit} = \text{Contribution} - \text{Fixed Costs}$$

$$\text{Break Even Point} = \frac{\text{Fixed Costs}}{\text{Unit Sales Price} - \text{Unit Variable Costs}}$$

Fixed Costs: The cost is fixed if it remains constant over a relevant range even when the volume of activity varies.

Variable Costs: The cost is variable if it changes when the volume of activity changes.

1. Compute sales, contribution, and net profit if product line E is eliminated.

   Sales _____

   Contribution _____

   Net Profit _____

2. After extensive evaluation, the marketing manager decided to modify product line D by raising the selling price 8%, putting a premium surcharge on small orders, and instructing the sales force not to spend much selling effort on product line D. With these modifications, the marketing manager estimated that the sales of product line D would be $3,000,000 with a contribution of $300,000. Compute sales, contribution, and net profit if product line E is eliminated and product line D is modified.

   Sales _____

   Contribution _____

   Net Profit _____

NAME _____

Exercise 13-1   PRODUCT AND SERVICE AUGMENTATION

There are three levels to thinking about a product. They are 1) the core product, 2) the tangible product, and 3) the augmented product. The core product is the basic problem satisfaction or benefits buyers want when they purchase; people do not want drills, they want the holes that drills provide. The tangible product is the means by which the problem is solved and may involve a quality level, features, styling, brands, and packaging. The augmented product reflects awareness of the buyers' total consumption systems and the suppliers' related marketing-mix elements that are likely to be valued in consumption systems such as repair services, financing, special delivery arrangements, etc.

Instruction: Read each of the following statements and indicate the product level involved. Select just one for each statement.

	Core Product	Tangible Product	Augmented Product
1. To make it easier for tourists to visit Disneyland and its adjacent Epcot Center, management opened a hotel on the resort property. The hotel is connected by monorail to the two amusement parks.	( )	( )	( )
2. Many of the sofas offered by Levitz Furniture Corp. feature olefin/nylon blend fabrics. Some have cushions that have reversible covers for extra-long wear.	( )	( )	( )
3. Godfather's, a fast-food chain that specializes in pizza, has recently added a delivery service.	( )	( )	( )
4. Many parents buy a set of World Book Encyclopedias in the hope that their children will learn more quickly and easily with this educational resource handy.	( )	( )	( )
5. The Reed Aluminum Siding Company sells aluminum siding to home owners. Management has instituted a long term credit purchase program in cooperation with leading institutions.	( )	( )	( )
6. Eastman Kodak is facing increased competition from foreign manufacturers of	( )	( )	( )

© 1986 by Prentice-Hall, A Division of Simon & Schuster, Inc.
Englewood Cliffs, N.J. 07632. All rights reserved.
Printed in the United States of America.

	Core Product	Tangible Product	Augmented Product

photographic film. To offset the sales effort of these competitors, Kodak has improved the brillance of its color film.

7. The Greater Phoenix Tourist Center promotes the number of days without rain as a tourist attraction of Phoenix. ( ) ( ) ( )

8. College professors prefer to think that students attend college to learn. ( ) ( ) ( )

9. The so-called Ivy League colleges promote their tradition and their quality to attract students to these generally costly institutions of learning. ( ) ( ) ( )

10. Many large Kroger "superstores" offer not only check cashing at their supermarkets but also limited banking services, delicatessen food, wines, pharmacies, flowers and valet delivery of grocery bags to the customer's automobile. ( ) ( ) ( )

11. Many car buyers seek excitement and power in automobiles. ( ) ( ) ( )

12. In order to stimulate new truck sales, Chuck Brown Chevrolet, a dealer in Columbia, Missouri, offered new Silverado pickup trucks at no down payment. In competition, Chad Williams Dodge offered custom paint jobs on all new trucks. ( ) ( ) ( )

13. Motion-picture producers release comedies and adventure films featuring juvenile actors during the summer. The producers believe the teenage market has the time and money during summer to respond to offers of light entertainment. ( ) ( ) ( )

14. CMC is a chain offering radios, stereos and video sets. CMC features a low-price guarantee. If you find your CMC purchase advertised for less money within 30 days, CMC will refund the difference plus 20% of the difference. ( ) ( ) ( )

Exercise 13-2   PRODUCT AND SERVICE AUGMENTATION

There are three levels to thinking about a product. They are 1) the core product, 2) the tangible product, and 3) the augmented product. The core product is the basic problem satisfaction or benefits buyers want when they purchase; people do not want drills, they want the holes that drills provide. The tangible product is the means by which the problem is solved and may involve a quality level, features, styling, brands, and packaging. The augmented product reflects awareness of the buyers' total consumption systems and the suppliers' related marketing mix elements that are likely to be valued in consumption systems, such as repair services, financing, special delivery arrangements, etc.

Instruction: Read each of the following statements and indicate the product level involved. Select just one for each statement.

	Core Product	Tangible Product	Augmented Product
1. All Hyatt Regency hotels offer flower shops, laundry and dry cleaning, and exhibit-hall space.	( )	( )	( )
2. Most buyers of government bonds are primarily seeking security.	( )	( )	( )
3. Carrier sells central air conditioners through a large distribution system. Carrier's dealers not only install units but also offer Carrier's 100% retail credit. Most dealers also sell Carrier's electronic air cleaner that can be attached to air conditioners.	( )	( )	( )
4. The AT&T PC C300 personal computer has 640 K RAM, graphics, parallel printer port, mouse port, real time clock, tilt and swivel green monitor, keyboard, and two 360 K floppy disk drives. In 1985 it sold for $1995.	( )	( )	( )
5. Buyers of fresh produce and fruits find them to be nourishing and healthful.	( )	( )	( )
6. Workbench is a chain of 56 stores in 17 states selling a wide variety of home furniture. According to its	( )	( )	( )

© 1986 by Prentice-Hall, A Division of Simon & Schuster, Inc.
Englewood Cliffs, N.J. 07632. All rights reserved.
Printed in the United States of America.

	Core Product	Tangible Product	Augmented Product

advertisements Workbench offers delivery within ten days, trained salespeople, and its own credit card.

7. Casual & Patio Furniture Company sells Samsonite patio and pool furniture. Samsonite's Body Glove line has a durable steel frame that is welded for extra strength. It is coated with a P.V.C. finish that resists chipping, scratching, and rust.　　( )　( )　( )

8. Brook Mays Music, a three-store retailer, offers musical instruments. Purchasers of pianos or organs during the summer of 1985 were eligible for Brook Mays' adult piano learning center course of nine weeks of private lessons.　　( )　( )　( )

9. Many purchasers of physical fitness equipment hope to achieve longer life.　　( )　( )　( )

10. Kitchen Aid manufactures a durable dishwasher. It has an exclusive triple filtration, a "hard" food disposer, porcelain-on-steel tank and inner door, and solid-state control panel.　　( )　( )　( )

11. Many autoists carry flashlights in their autos' glove compartments for safety.　　( )　( )　( )

12. Lite Fantastic, a retail store in Chicago, offers lighting fixtures and fans. It sells Casablanca Fan Company's Delta II fan. It is complete with tulip four-light kit, 52" blades, five-speed switch, a patented "Hang-Tru" ceiling mount, and a choice of polished or antique brass finishes.　　( )　( )　( )

13. Some purchasers of grandfather-type clocks hope to provide a gracious, traditional atmosphere to the entry halls of their homes.　　( )　( )　( )

Exercise 13-3   PRODUCT AND SERVICE AUGMENTATION

There are three levels to thinking about a product. They are 1) the core product, 2) the tangible product, and 3) the augmented product. The core product is the basic problem satisfaction or benefits buyers want when they purchase; people do not want drills, they want the holes that drills provide. The tangible product is the means by which the problem is solved and may involve a quality level, features, styling, brands, and packaging. The augmented product reflects awareness of the buyers' total consumption systems and the suppliers' related marketing mix elements that are likely to be valued in consumption systems such as repair services, financing, special delivery arrangements, etc.

> Instruction: Read each of the following statements and indicate the product level involved. Select just one for each statement.

	Core Product	Tangible Product	Augmented Product
1. To assist new college graduates in purchasing its autos, General Motors Acceptance Corp. arranges financing to graduates who can show proof of pending employment. GMAC requires no down payment and no monthly payments for 90 days.	( )	( )	(✓)
2. IBM ran an advertisement in the Wall Street Journal stating, "After helping you choose a computer, your IBM representative will help you with financing."	( )	( )	(✓)
3. Amtrak, the federally subsidized passenger railroad, projected a 4% increase in ridership for its 1985 year. Its train Southwest Chief, which runs between Chicago and Los Angeles, has added movies, bingo, regional drinks, and lectures by an Indian guide.	( )	( )	(✓)
4. Business travelers prefer airline travel over competing modes. They value the speed and reliability.	(✓)	( )	( )
5. Regency Air Corp. offers one eastbound and one westbound flight daily between New York and London. The ticket price is $785 one-way. The	( )	( )	(✓)

© 1986 by Prentice-Hall, A Division of Simon & Schuster, Inc.
Englewood Cliffs, N.J. 07632. All rights reserved.
Printed in the United States of America.

	Core Product	Tangible Product	Augmented Product

price includes door-to-door limo service, a hairdresser, a manicurist, secretarial service, conference rooms and bedrooms.

6. Wendy's International has positioned itself to market primarily to adults. In addition to offering quality hamburgers, it also has its Light Side salad menu and baked potatoes.
( )   (✓)   ( )

7. BMW automobiles are identified by many as a symbol of the young, upwardly mobile, professional group. Some demographers apply the label "yuppies" to those individuals.
(✓)   ( )   ( )

8. Some consumers desire a quick energy food pickup between meals. Executives at Mars, Inc., have repositioned Snickers candy bar advertising to fit this snack food category.
(✓)   ( )   ( )

9. Red Lobster restaurants are part of General Mill's Restaurant Group. When profits fell slightly in 1984, management spent $104 million to refurbish their 373 units nationwide. Changes included adding oyster bars, mesquite grills, and a new, more varied menu. Lighter foods, including snacks, are featured.
( )   ( )   ( )

10. To compete with hotels, some enterprising individuals offer bed and breakfast inns. These are generally restored old homes owned by the operators. Rooms are frequently uniquely decorated with antique furniture, and breakfasts are included in the price of the room.
( )   ( )   ( )

11. Credit cards supply their users with a substitute for cash.
(✓)   ( )   ( )

12. When a guest stays at the Four Seasons hotel in Houston, the guest is entitled to use the facilities of the Houston Center Health Club next door.
( )   ( )   (✓)

Exercise 14-1   CLASSIFICATION OF CONSUMER GOODS

   A useful way to classify the vast range of consumer goods available
for purchase is to divide them into the categories of 1) convenience,
2) shopping, 3) specialty, and 4) unsought goods. This classification is
based on the way people buy. <u>Convenience goods</u> are purchased frequently
and with a minimum of effort. If the customer's favorite brand is out of
stock, the customer will quickly settle for a substitute. In contrast,
<u>shopping goods</u> are purchased infrequently, and generally only after com-
parison of such merits as quality, price, or style. <u>Specialty goods</u> are
those that have such unique characteristics that buyers are willing to make
a special effort to secure them. <u>Unsought goods</u> are those that the
individual does not know about or knows about but does not have a strong
interest in purchasing.

          Instruction: Read each of the following statements
          and indicate which category is involved. Select
          just one for each statement.

	Conve- nience goods	Shopping goods	Spe- cialty goods	Unsought goods
1. You have been told by a very knowl- edgeable computer major that you should buy an old Osborne portable computer, if you can locate one. You phone 47 computer stores with- out success but you still have another 20 on your list.	( )	( )	( )	( )
2. You receive an unexpected sales call by a door-to-door salesperson offering credit terms on the pre- purchase of a gravestone.	( )	( )	( )	( )
3. A case of Coor's beer is brought back to campus by a college student returning from Thanksgiving break. Coor's is not distributed in the state where the student's univer- sity is located.	( )	( )	( )	( )
4. You buy a pack of cigarettes. You purchase it from a retail store on the route between your room and your classroom.	( )	( )	( )	( )
5. A can of Coca Cola is purchased from a courtside vending machine by a college senior to refresh	( )	( )	( )	( )

© 1986 by Prentice-Hall, A Division of Simon & Schuster, Inc.
Englewood Cliffs, N.J. 07632. All rights reserved.
Printed in the United States of America.

	Conve- nience goods	Shopping goods	Spe- cialty goods	Unsought goods

himself after a fast game of tennis on a hot day.

6. A bald individual is awakened from an afternoon's nap by a door-to-door salesperson selling Fuller hair brushes.   ( )   ( )   ( )   ( )

7. The case of Coor's beer brought back to campus above is raffled off by your dormitory. The winner is an individual who abstains from alcohol.   ( )   ( )   ( )   ( )

8. You purchase from a nearby store a copy of the Cleveland Plain Dealer newspaper for the purpose of determining which theaters are showing a particular film.   ( )   ( )   ( )   ( )

9. Joe Brady desires a reliable used car with low mileage that can be used for the purpose of daily driving to work. He plans to visit several used car lots.   ( )   ( )   ( )   ( )

10. Your sister insists on the Clinique brand of cosmetics. It is manufactured for individuals who are allergic to ingredients in normal cosmetics.   ( )   ( )   ( )   ( )

11. A friend purchased a new Oldsmobile Cutlass automobile from the Bill McDavid Olds dealership after trips to Mossy Olds and Rice-Menger Olds to compare deals.   ( )   ( )   ( )   ( )

12. Betty needed a five-pound package of granulated sugar for general use as a sweetner in the home. After looking at several brands, Betty selected the store brand because of its lower price.   ( )   ( )   ( )   ( )

NAME *Joseph Troper*

Exercise 14-2   CLASSIFICATION OF CONSUMER GOODS

A useful way to classify the vast range of consumer goods available for purchase is to divide them into the categories of 1) convenience, 2) shopping, 3) specialty, and 4) unsought goods. This classification is based on the way people buy. <u>Convenience goods</u> are purchased frequently and with a minimum of effort. If the customer's favorite brand is out of stock, the customer will quickly settle for a substitute. In contrast, <u>shopping goods</u> are purchased infrequently, and generally only after comparison of such merits as quality, price, or style. <u>Specialty goods</u> are those that have such unique characteristics that buyers are willing to make a special effort to secure them. <u>Unsought goods</u> are those that the individual does not know about or knows about but does not have a strong interest in purchasing.

Instruction: Read each of the following statements and indicate which category is involved. Select just one for each statement.

	Convenience goods	Shopping goods	Specialty goods	Unsought goods
1. A purchase of three Ralph Lauren's Polo brand blue oxford cloth shirts with button-down collars is made by an individual who insists upon Polo brand shirts.	( )	( )	(✓)	( )
2. Macy's department store stocks General Electric, Westinghouse, and Frigidaire brands of refrigerators at its downtown store as well as in its branch stores located in major shopping malls so that buyers can compare features.	( )	(✓)	( )	( )
3. After obtaining a price quotation on a new Ford Motor Co. Merkur XR4Ti car at Brown's Lincoln-Mercury dealership, you attempt to obtain a competitive price quotation at another Ford dealership and find that only a few Mercury dealers stock them.	( )	( )	( )	( )
4. Through a computer error, the president of your college marketing club receives 200 identical direct mail pieces describing the attributes of a nursing home for elderly, retired	( )	( )	( )	(✓)

© 1986 by Prentice-Hall, A Division of Simon & Schuster, Inc. Englewood Cliffs, N.J. 07632. All rights reserved. Printed in the United States of America.

	Conve-nience goods	Shopping goods	Spe-cialty goods	Unsought goods

railroad workers.

5. Tom Sims wishes to buy a suit for graduation. He visits a major department store where he finds Pierre Cardin, Oxxford, Hart, Shaffner and Marx, and Johnny Carson brand suits.

( )   (✔)   ( )   (✔)

6. Students can buy Marlboro brand cigarettes from coin-operated vending machines. The machines are located in university dining halls and dormitories.

( )   ( )   ( )   ( )

7. Several police officers at the Hill Street Station have notified their buddies that, in case the officers are injured in line of duty, they wish to be taken to Presbyterian Hospital for treatment. Although the Presbyterian Hospital may not be the nearest emergency room, it has the most complete facilities, including around-the-clock staffing by a team of trauma specialists.

( )   ( )   ( )   ( )

8. A twenty-volume set of World Book encyclopedias is offered by a salesman to a single male college senior.

( )   ( )   ( )   (✔)

9. As customers go through the checkout lines at Kroger's, they can buy Baby Ruth candy bars that are on display at the cash register.

( )   ( )   ( )   ( )

10. The combined offer from a door-to-door salesperson of funeral home and cemetery services at a special price is made available for preneed purchase to your healthy seventeen-year-old nephew.

( )   ( )   ( )   ( )

11. Tony Lama brand ostrich-skin, dress cowboy boots are available at either of the two Cutter Bill's Western Wear shops in town for buyers who prefer this unique texture and quality.

( )   ( )   ( )   ( )

NAME _____

Exercise 14-3   CLASSIFICATION OF CONSUMER GOODS

A useful way to classify the vast range of consumer goods available for purchase is to divide them into the categories of 1) convenience, 2) shopping, 3) specialty, and 4) unsought goods. This classification is based on the way people buy. <u>Convenience goods</u> are purchased frequently and with a minimum of effort. If the customer's favorite brand is out of stock, the customer will quickly settle for a substitute. In contrast, <u>shopping goods</u> are purchased infrequently, and generally only after comparison of such merits as quality, price, or style. <u>Specialty goods</u> are those that have such unique characteristics that buyers are willing to make a special effort to secure them. <u>Unsought goods</u> are those that the individual does not know about or knows about but does not have a strong interest in purchasing.

Instruction: Read each of the following statements and indicate which category is involved. Select just one for each statement.

	Convenience goods	Shopping goods	Specialty goods	Unsought goods
1. Upon noticing that it is raining, your favorite professor stops by the campus bookstore to purchase an umbrella on his way to class.	( )	( )	( )	( )
2. After learning from your mother that your favorite aunt would like a new umbrella for her birthday, you borrow your roommate's car and drive to a major department store, where you select an attractive women's umbrella at a price you can afford.	( )	( )	( )	( )
3. Your least favorite cousin, whom you have disliked from childhood, upstages your gift by giving your aunt a very rare old umbrella of silk, complete with a silver handle dating from Queen Victoria's time. He sought it out for her in a shop in England devoted to unusual umbrellas.	( )	( )	( )	( )
4. You are on your way to take an exam and realize that you are without a writing instrument. You purchase a pencil at the campus bookstore on your way to class.	( )	( )	( )	( )

© 1986 by Prentice-Hall, A Division of Simon & Schuster, Inc.
Englewood Cliffs, N.J. 07632. All rights reserved.
Printed in the United States of America.

	Conve-nience goods	Shopping goods	Spe-cialty goods	Unsought goods

5. After the exam is over, you drive to a major shopping center to look over the selection of pens and pencils. After considerable review of the many items available, you select a more suitable one. ( ) ( ) ( ) ( )

6. Your aunt, having sold the rare umbrella for a large sum, insists on purchasing a fountain pen that uses bottled ink. She desires a pen similar to those that were available when she was young. It also must write a very fine line. ( ) ( ) ( ) ( )

7. Your cousin has graduated from college and now sells life insurance. He suggests that although you are just completing your junior year in college and are paying your own way, you should purchase a life-insurance policy. ( ) ( ) ( ) ( )

8. Your cousin also informs you that he has learned that NASA is now selling tickets for future flights to the moon. He would like you to accompany him and he offers to pay 50% of your fare. In the past, you have avoided flying because you become airsick.

8. A direct-mail ad is received by an advocate of gun control. It features sale prices on revolvers at Barley's House of Guns, Inc. ( ) ( ) ( ) ( )

10. An offensive tackle on the Ohio State University football team searches for a store that stocks Ban brand underarm deodorant. He is convinced that Ban is the only one that works for him. ( ) ( ) ( ) ( )

11. A customer purchases Ban brand underarm deodorant at a nearby campus store. The purchaser normally uses Sure brand, but the store was out of stock. ( ) ( ) ( ) ( )

Exercise 15-1   INDUSTRIAL GOODS AND SERVICES

Three tpes of industrial goods and services are 1) materials and parts, 2) capital items, and 3) supplies and services. <u>Materials and parts</u> become part of the final product. Raw materials are unprocessed primary materials, such as iron ore, crude petroleum, or wheat. Parts can be either finished component items purchased ready for assembly into the finished product or parts that need further processing before assembly. <u>Capital items</u> may be major installations, such as a large stamping machine; or may be smaller, of a shorter life span, and less expensive, such as electric typewriters or table saws. <u>Supplies and services</u> do not become part of the final item nor are they utilized in the production process. Supplies are convenience items that are sometimes referred to as MRO items because they include maintenance, repair, and operating supplies. Services, on the other hand, are intangible items, such as engineering, consulting, and legal services.

Instructions: Read each of the following statements and indicate which category is primarily involved. Select just one for each statement.

	Materials and Parts	Capital Items	Supplies and Services
1. J&N Sales Company sells POW'R GARD brand gasoline and diesel powered generators for industrial use as the standby, emergency generator of electricity.	( )	( )	( )
2. Adolph Coors, brewer of Coors beer, has emphasized in its promotional programs the quality of the water it uses for brewing beer, saying "It's not downstream beer."	( )	( )	( )
3. Epcot Center, the $1 billion Disney development in Florida, relied heavily on a Sperry Univac computer to operate its many displays and electronic figures.	( )	( )	( )
4. The Illinois Window Cleaning Company offers business firms complete window washing by workmen who are fully bonded and insured.	( )	( )	( )
5. Hendricks Chemical Corp. uses the chemical isopropanol as the main ingredient in its manufacture of rubbing alcohol. Hendricks purchases	( )	( )	( )

© 1986 by Prentice-Hall, A Division of Simon & Schuster, Inc.
Englewood Cliffs, N.J. 07632. All rights reserved.
Printed in the United States of America.

	Materials and Parts	Capital Items	Supplies and services

isopropanol from the Allied Chemical Corporation in tank car amounts.

6. Westchester Steel Corporation had to shut down its Youngstown, Ohio, steel rolling mill while installing newly designed drives that powered the rolls. The new drives provided a higher degree of precision in the finish of steel processed through the mill.

( ) ( ) ( )

7. Grimes Bookkeeping systems, under the slogan, "Your place or mine," specializes in small business tax services for partnerships and small corporations.

( ) ( ) ( )

8. West Bend Wire and Cable Company of Ohio supplies manufacturers of electric motors with a wide variety of wiring for use in the production of motors.

( ) ( ) ( )

9. Southwest Landscape Control Company offers businesses complete landscape care, including weed control, fertilizing, pruning, and mowing. The firm also has a golf-course design department.

( ) ( ) ( )

10. Frog Design, Inc. specializes in designing the exterior appearance and casings for electronic products; its design for the Apple IIc computer was highly regarded.

( ) ( ) ( )

11. The Navy, ending a decade during which Grumman built replacement wings for the Grumman A-6E airplane, selected Boeing Co. in 1985 to design and produce the wings. They will be made of graphite epoxy.

( ) ( ) ( )

12. According to GBS, a consulting firm, 35% of small business computers end up gathering dust because they turn out not to be the appropriate model for the buyers' needs.

( ) ( ) ( )

Exercise 15-2   INDUSTRIAL GOODS AND SERVICES

Three types of industrial goods and services are 1) materials and parts, 2) capital items, and 3) supplies and services. <u>Materials and parts</u> become part of the final product. Raw materials are unprocessed primary materials, such as iron ore, crude petroleum, or wheat. Parts can be either finished component items purchased ready for assembly into the finished product, or parts that need further processing before assembly. <u>Capital items</u> may be major installations, such as a large stamping machine; or may be smaller, of a shorter life span, and less expensive, such as electric typewriters or table saws. <u>Supplies and services</u> do not become part of the final item nor are they utilized in the production process. Supplies are convenience items that are sometimes referred to as MRO items because they include maintenance, repair, and operating supplies. Services, on the other hand, are intangible items, such as engineering, consulting, and legal services.

Instructions: Read each of the following statements and indicate which category is primarily involved. Select just one for each statement.

	Materials and Parts	Capital Items	Supplies and Services
1. General Electric Company has established a factory automation planning service to sell advice to corporate customers on how they can make their plants more efficient with numerical controls, robots, computers for design and manufacturing, automated order entry, and warehousing systems.	( )	( )	( )
2. Marimon Business Machine Company, a wholesale distributor of office stationery, legal forms, writing instruments, and paper clips, is attempting to satisfy the needs of the G.E. plant located in St. Louis.	( )	( )	( )
3. The cost to the General Electric Company of installing robots in its Louisville, Kentucky, appliance plant was $38 million.	( )	( )	( )
4. General Electric has begun marketing to other firms a line of robots that do assembly, printing, or welding.	( )	( )	( )
5. It is the policy of General Electric to manufacture the small electric	( )	( )	( )

© 1986 by Prentice-Hall, A Division of Simon & Schuster, Inc. Englewood Cliffs, N.J. 07632. All rights reserved. Printed in the United States of America.

	Materials and Parts	Capital Items	Supplies and Services

motors that are used in its line of consumer items, such as fans, refrigerators, and hair dryers, rather than purchase them from outside vendors.

	Materials and Parts	Capital Items	Supplies and Services
6. The amount of wire used annually by GE in its electric motor divisions would reach to the moon and back.	( )	( )	( )
7. Hill and Knowlton, Inc., is a national public relations agency that has among its clients major competitors of GE.	( )	( )	( )
8. GE, after sending RFQ's (requisitions for quotations) to three suppliers specifying bids on a chemical mixer making plant resins, placed an order with one of the firms.	( )	( )	( )
9. GE makes extensive use of thermoplastics for product cases and handles. It purchases the thermoplastics in pellet form in large quantities from several suppliers and plants.	( )	( )	( )
10. In 1985, Apple Computer, Inc., was negotiating with other manufacturers to supply a file server and the necessary hard-disk drives under its label to further its entrance into the office-equipment market.	( )	( )	( )
11. Computervision Corp., which had been providing programs linking a variety of computers with its mainstay microcomputer, the CDS 4000, will now provide software that may be run on desktop computers.	( )	( )	( )
12. Ford Motor Co., which owns 25% of Mazda, will buy engines from the Japanese automaker for a sporty subcompact it plans to build in 1988 at a new $500 million plant in Hermosillo, Mexico. Evaluate the engine purchase.	( )	( )	( )

Exercise 15-3   INDUSTRIAL GOODS AND SERVICES

Three types of industrial goods and services are 1) materials and parts, 2) capital items, and 3) supplies and services. <u>Materials and parts</u> become part of the final product. Raw materials are unprocessed primary materials, such as iron ore, crude petroleum, or wheat. Parts can be either finished component items purchased ready for assembly into the finished product or parts that need further processing before assembly. <u>Capital items</u> may be major installations, such as a large stamping machine; or may be smaller, of a shorter life span, and less expensive, such as electric typewriters or table saws. <u>Supplies and services</u> do not become part of the final item nor are they utilized in the production process. Supplies are convenience items that are sometimes referred to as MRO items because they include maintenance, repair, and operating supplies. Services, on the other hand, are intangible items, such as engineering, consulting, and legal services.

Instructions: Read each of the following statements and indicate which category is primarily involved. Select just one for each statement.

	Materials and Parts	Capital Items	Supplies and Services
1. In its large nine-million-barrel capacity brewery in Milwaukee, Wisconsin, Miller Brewing Company has six high-speed canning and bottling machines.	( )	( )	( )
2. The Miller brewing process begins with malt that is obtained from barley. The major purchases of barley are made in California, the Dakotas, and Minnesota.	( )	( )	( )
3. Janitorial services at all of the Miller breweries are costly, since management demands clean plants.	( )	( )	( )
4. Miller Brewing Company uses a strain of yeast first cultivated in Germany hundreds of years ago and brought to the U.S. by Frederick Miller in 1855.	( )	( )	( )
5. The copper brew kettles in which water, malt, corn, and hops are boiled were custom-made for Miller.	( )	( )	( )
6. Miller buys a wide variety of office supplies from a number of different	( )	( )	( )

© 1986 by Prentice-Hall, A Division of Simon & Schuster, Inc.
Englewood Cliffs, N.J. 07632. All rights reserved.
Printed in the United States of America.

	Materials and Parts	Capital Items	Supplies and Services

office-supply companies on a bid
basis.

7. Hops, responsible for the aroma and bitterness in beer, are obtained only from flowers from the female hop plant. The hops are grown primarily in Oregon and California.	( )	( )	( )
8. In addition to its headquarters plant, Miller has breweries in Texas, North Carolina, New York, California, Georgia, and Ohio. Each brewery has $600,000 in quality-control equipment.	( )	( )	( )
9. Each production area of each brewery is kept clean and hosed down daily with a powerful stream of water.	( )	( )	( )
10. Tabulating Systems and Service, Inc., an accounting services firm, purchased a 16,760-square-foot office and warehouse in Missouri City, Texas, near the Texas brewery of one of its clients, Miller. Evaluate TS&S's action.	( )	( )	( )
11. After the Phillip Morris Company purchased the Miller Brewing Company, PM introduced a novel advertising campaign that established Miller Lite as the nation's best-selling light beer.	( )	( )	( )
12. In spite of outlays of large amounts of advertising funds, sales of Miller's regular brand, Miller High Life, continued to decline for a number of years.	( )	( )	( )
13. Although Adolf Coors, one of Miller's major competitors, ships its beer in refrigerated trucks, Miller's fleet of trucks is not refrigerated.	( )	( )	( )

Exercise 16-1   BRANDING ALTERNATIVES

Three major types of branding alternatives used in the marketplace are 1) manufacturer brands, 2) dealer brands, and 3) generic brands. <u>Manufacturer brands</u> are sponsored by a manufacturer and are usually well known and heavily promoted. They are frequently called national brands. <u>Private brands</u> are sponsored by wholesalers or retailers. Dealers normally give extensive shelf space to these brands. These brands are frequently called dealer brands. <u>Generic brands</u> do not have a brand name separate from the name of the product. Generic products are sold at a low price and receive little promotion.

Instructions: Read each of the following statements and indicate which brands are involved. Select only one category.

	Manufacturer Brands	Private Brands	Generic Brands
1. Houstonian, desiring to dominate the $46 billion fitness industry, recently acquired Elaine Powers Figure Salons and will change the name to Living Well Fitness Centers. In its centers, Houstonian markets a 120-item line from leotards to dietary supplements.	( )	( )	( )
2. Honda, which holds about 80% of the motor scooter market, featured a TV commercial with Lou Reed. The background music is from Reed's funky 1972 song about a transvestite, entitled "Walk on the Wild Side."	( )	( )	( )
3. Private Label brand cigarettes have recently been introduced by a tobacco manufacturer with regional advertising support. Sales have been limited.	( )	( )	( )
4. No-name tea bags are sold by a number of supermarket chains. These tea bags do not have tags and are stuffed into plastic pouches.	( )	( )	( )
5. Rock and Roll beer was introduced in 1982 by Joe Edwards, who owns a tavern in St. Louis. Mr. Edwards promotes his house beer, which he buys from the Dixie Brewery Company.	( )	( )	( )

© 1986 by Prentice-Hall, A Division of Simon & Schuster, Inc.
Englewood Cliffs, N.J. 07632. All rights reserved.
Printed in the United States of America.

	Manufacturer Brands	Private Brands	Generic Brands
6. King Supers is the biggest supermarket chain in Denver. The largest-selling paper towel in Denver is the chain's three-year-old product, labeled simply "Paper Towels."	( )	( )	( )
7. Philip Morris produces and heavily advertises Virginia Slims cigarettes. The primary market for the cigarettes is women.	( )	( )	( )
8. Safeway Supermarkets promotes its Lucerne brand of milk and dairy products heavily in its stores. Generally, Safeway allocates most of its shelf space in the dairy section to Lucerne brands.	( )	( )	( )
9. Elmer's Glue is a strong brand of glue that Borden's has successfully promoted over a long period of time.	( )	( )	( )
10. J. C. Penney promotes its Penney's brand of portable televisions to the general public. Penney's buys some of these TV sets directly from Panasonic.	( )	( )	( )
11. Rohm and Haas Chemical Company sells its Plexiglas brand of cell-cast acrylic sheets to plastic distributors and acrylic sheet-end users.	( )	( )	( )
12. Heinz, whose mustard had a much smaller market share than the market leader French's, dropped marketing efforts on the West Coast and concentrated in the Midwest and East.	( )	( )	( )
13. In order to keep its plants operating closer to capacity, Borden's manufactures lower margin generics.	( )	( )	( )

NAME *Joseph Lopez*

Exercise 16-2   BRANDING ALTERNATIVES

Three major types of branding alternatives used in the marketplace are 1) manufacturer brands, 2) dealer brands, and 3) generic brands. <u>Manufacturer brands</u> are sponsored by a manufacturer, and are usually well known and heavily promoted. They are frequently called national brands. <u>Private brands</u> are sponsored by wholesalers or retailers. Dealers normally give extensive shelf space to these brands. These brands are frequently called dealer brands. <u>Generic brands</u> do not have a brand name separate from the name of the product. Generic products are sold at a low price and receive little promotion.

Instructions: Read each of the following statements and indicate which brands are involved. Select only one category.

	Manufacturer Brands	Private Brands	Generic Brands
1. Beatrice/Hunt-Wesson Foods company attempted to reposition its ailing Sunlite sunflower-oil brand by changing the name to Sunlite Wesson 100% Sun-flower Seed Oil.	(✓)	( )	( )
2. Jewel Stores Co., a Midwest grocery store chain with 217 stores, shut down its Hillfarm brand milk-processing plant and pulled all of its milk products immediately from store shelves after public health authorities found that one batch of its Bluebrook 2% milk contained salmonella bacteria.	( )	( )	( )
3. Nabisco Brands manufactures and promotes a wide range of food products. Its Nabisco cookies and crackers have maintained a high share of the market for the last 20 years in spite of competition from Duncan Hines, Keeblers, and others.	( )	( )	( )
4. Pathmark Supermarkets introduced no-frills food and household products in 1978. On the average these items sold for 33% less than the chain's own private label items.	( )	( )	(✓)
5. Topco, a large food wholesaler, promotes its Food Club brand of food products in a number of local and regional supermarket	( )	( )	( )

© 1986 by Prentice-Hall, A Division of Simon & Schuster, Inc.
Englewood Cliffs, N.J. 07632. All rights reserved.
Printed in the United States of America.

	Manufac-turer Brands	Private Brands	Generic Brands

chains.

6. Many physicians now prescribe penicillin to their patients where appropriate. Druggists sell this widely used antibiotic drug to many customers who have the required prescriptions.

| | ( ) | ( ) | (✓) |

7. Sears has spent millions of dollars over a number of years promoting its Die-Hard battery.

| | ( ) | ( ) | ( ) |

8. In the last few years, Miller Brewing Company has had outstanding success in its introduction of Lite beer. The TV commercials have won a number of advertising awards.

| | (✓) | ( ) | ( ) |

9. Hudson Oil Company is a large chain of retail service stations. It promotes and sells its Hudson brand of gasoline in a number of states.

| | ( ) | ( ) | ( ) |

10. Although Union Carbide is primarily identified with the chemical industry, it has developed a number of strong consumer products. Glad trash bags are strongly promoted by Union Carbide to all types of consumers.

| | ( ) | ( ) | ( ) |

11. When Germany's Albrecht Group opened its first Aldi grocery store in the United States, rather than stocking the typical 12,000 varieties of items, the store stocked only one brand and size in only 500 categories at a 20% reduction in prices. The brands were known in the U.S.

| | ( ) | ( ) | ( ) |

12. J. C. Penney has been repositioning itself by moving away from a private label, price-conscious general merchandiser to a more moderately priced, higher-fashion department store for upper-middle-income families.

| | ( ) | (✓) | ( ) |

102

Exercise 16-3   BRANDING ALTERNATIVES

Three major types of branding alternatives used in the marketplace are
1) manufacturer brands, 2) dealer brands, and 3) generic brands. <u>Manufac-
turer brands</u> are sponsored by a manufacturer, and are usually well known and
heavily promoted. They are frequently called national brands. <u>Private
brands</u> are sponsored by wholesalers or retailers. Dealers normally give
extensive shelf space to these brands. These brands are frequently called
dealer brands. <u>Generic brands</u> do not have a brand name separate from the
name of the product. Generic products are sold at a low price and receive
little promotion.

Instructions: Read each of the following statements
and indicate which brands are involved. Select only
one category.

	Manufac-turer Brands	Private Brands	Generic Brands
1. Biological Controls of California offers exclusive licenses to investors for $7500 to Roach Musk 7, the brand name of a new roach-killing substance. Licensees purchase the rights to franchise other distributors in their area. Roach Musk 7 sells at retail for $199 and emits a sex scent that attracts roaches.	( )	( )	( )
2. Coors Light, which broke a 20-year company tradition of brewing only one beer when it was introduced in 1978, has become the beer industry's no. 2 light beer behind Miller Lite.	( )	( )	( )
3. American International Rent A Car is utilizing a cartoon character of a pencil-toting bespectacled dog to visualize lower rates in addition to the normal brand name. The firm ranks sixth in the franchise car rental business.	( )	( )	( )
4. Ralph's Grocery Company in Southern California sells a wide range of grocery products identified as "Plain Wrap." These products are priced cheaper than both national and private brands.	( )	( )	( )
5. The A&P Supermarket chain has promoted and given a large amount of shelf space	( )	( )	( )

© 1986 by Prentice-Hall, A Division of Simon & Schuster, Inc.
Englewood Cliffs, N.J. 07632. All rights reserved.
Printed in the United States of America.

	Manufacturer Brands	Private Brands	Generic Brands

to its Ann Page brand of food products.

6. Outboard Marine Company manufactures and heavily promotes its Evinrude brand motors for both inboard and outboard boats.   ( )   ( )   ( )

7. Rexall Company started out as a drug wholesaler. It was very successful in promoting its Rexall brand drug through independent retail druggists.   ( )   ( )   ( )

8. Kimberly-Clark produces a large group of consumer products. One of its major brands is Kleenex, which continues to dominate the facial-tissue market.   ( )   ( )   ( )

9. French Company manufactures and sells French Mustard. This strong brand of mustard has consistently sold well in the grocery stores.   ( )   ( )   ( )

10. Plain label brands of shredded wheat cereal are sold by the Stop and Shop Supermarket chain for almost 30% less than the national brands.   ( )   ( )   ( )

11. The Neiman-Marcus department store in Texas promotes and sells a lot of soft goods, such as shirts and blouses, under its Neiman-Marcus label.   ( )   ( )   ( )

12. The president of King Supers, Inc., the biggest supermarket chain in Denver, boasts that the largest selling paper towel in his city is not Bounty, the national market leader, but his chain's product labeled simply Paper Towels.   ( )   ( )   ( )

13. Robert T. Sakowitz, chairman of the 10-state Sakowitz specialty chain, announced that, after discussions with designer Halston about the proliferation of his label in competing stores, Halston will design some things exclusively for Sakowitz.   ( )   ( )   ( )

Exercise 17-1   PRODUCT LIFE CYCLE

The typical product or service is thought to move through an S-shaped sales curve from its introduction to its removal from the market. The four distinct stages in this movement are 1) introduction, 2) growth, 3) maturity, and 4) decline. The introduction stage is a period of slow sales growth, as it takes time for customers to learn about the product's availability and features. Production and marketing costs are high relative to the small number of sales because of the lack of mass-production economies. If the product survives the first stage by gaining market acceptance, it moves into the growth stage. In the growth stage, sales grow substantially and many companies enter the market. Promotion switches from emphasizing primary demand to a focus on selective demand stimulation. In the maturity stage, industry sales level off. Many managers compete in this stage through target market modification, product modification, or marketing mix modification. A substantial and permanent drop in the sales marks the decline stage. If any promotion is done, it is highly selective.

The product life cycle can be applied to a product class (toothpaste), product form (liquid toothpaste drops), or a brand (Pepsodent).

Instructions: Read each of the following statements and indicate which stage is primarily involved.

	Intro-duction	Growth	Matu-rity	De-cline
1. After ten years of poor profits, Banquet Foods was sold by RCA Corp. in 1980. The new owner, Con Agra, with its knowledge of agribusiness, reduced the mortality rates of chicks, improved quality control, and reduced costs. Sales stabilized and profits increased.	( )	( )	( )	( )
2. TSC Graphic's annual gross has now reached $100,000 and is continuing to grow. The company photographs marathon runners who finish in the six major U.S. marathons. A crew of twelve send rough proofs to all finishers. About one-third respond with an average purchase of $12. The founder is expanding to bicycle races, golf tournaments, swimming meets, and track events, where sales are also increasing. Competitors using videotapes are already entering the field.	( )	( )	( )	( )
3. In 1979, when the Houston Oilers faced the Pittsburgh Steelers on a Monday	( )	( )	( )	( )

© 1986 by Prentice-Hall, A Division of Simon & Schuster, Inc.
Englewood Cliffs, N.J. 07632. All rights reserved.
Printed in the United States of America.   105

	Intro-duction	Growth	Matu-rity	De-cline

night televised football game at the Astrodome, three little words "Luv Ya Blue!" shared the limelight. That slogan, attached to souvenirs, was expected to produce $7 million in sales, with $400,000 going to the Oilers. More than 135 different items were licensed for the slogan. In 1981, sales of "Luv Ya Blue!" items subsided sharply. In all, the Houston Oilers received only $50,000 in fees.

4. Two California entrepreneurs have developed a men's cologne called STASH that smells like marijuana. It costs $20 for a 3.75-ounce bottle. The ads do not mention marijuana, but a marijuana leaf is depicted on each bottle. Sales have not yet developed sufficiently to forecast future demand.

( ) ( ) ( ) ( )

5. For years, Proctor & Gamble has maintained sales of Ivory soap by promoting it as a gentle soap for washing babies. With the decline in births, P&G switched in 1971 to promoting Ivory for adults and continued its high level of sales.

( ) ( ) ( ) ( )

6. Although introduced only in May of 1982, by that fall Eastman Kodak's new line of disc cameras was pronounced a success by industry analysts. They take clearer, sharper pictures, and are so automatic that there is little opportunity for failure. Observers wondered only if the high price would restrict sales, but consumers responded rapidly.

( ) ( ) ( ) ( )

7. To enable you to start your car without leaving your bed, Audiovox Corp. of Hauppaunge, N.Y., sells the $325 Japanese-made Computer-Start. It turns your engine on and warms it up. It can also shut the engine off. Since its introduction, sales have been slow.

( ) ( ) ( ) ( )

Exercise 17-2   PRODUCT LIFE CYCLE

The typical product or service is thought to move through an S-shaped sales curve from its introduction to its removal from the market. The four distinct stages in this movement are 1) introduction, 2) growth, 3) maturity, and 4) decline. The introduction stage is a period of slow sales growth, as it takes time for customers to learn about the product's availability and features. Production and marketing costs are high relative to the small number of sales because of the lack of mass-production economies. If the product survives the first stage by gaining market acceptance, it moves into the growth stage. In the growth stage, sales grow substantially and many companies enter the market. Promotion switches from emphasizing primary demand to a focus on selective demand stimulation. In the maturity stage, industry sales level off. Many managers compete in this stage through target market modification, product modification, or marketing mix modification. A substantial and permanent drop in the sales marks the decline stage. If any promotion is done, it is highly selective.

The product life cycle can be applied to a product class (toothpaste), product form (liquid toothpaste drops), or a brand (Pepsodent).

Instructions: Read each of the following statements and indicate which stage is primarily involved.

	Intro-duction	Growth	Matu-rity	De-cline
1. In the early 1970s, automobile and truck drivers discovered citizens'-band radios, and a fad developed. A saturation level on the radio bands was soon reached and interest subsided rapidly. Many retailers were caught with substantial inventories.	( )	( )	( )	( )
2. The West-Tech Corp. marketed an electronic automobile horn for $69 that played popular tunes when pressed. A separate electronic attachment was required for each song played. They sold for $4.95 each and had to be ordered. Sales were increasing rapidly until a competitor marketed a unit for $79 that played any of 76 popular songs without attachments. Sales of the West-Tech product R-2 dropped. Evaluate West-Tech.	( )	( )	( )	( )
3. Del Monte Corporation is the nation's largest canner of fruits and vegetables. Increased production costs, declining	( )	( )	( )	( )

© 1986 by Prentice-Hall, A Division of Simon & Schuster, Inc.
Englewood Cliffs, N.J. 07632. All rights reserved.
Printed in the United States of America.

	Intro-duction	Growth	Matu-rity	De-cline

family size, and competition from frozen and fresh items have resulted in the canning business's losing its status as a growth industry as production levels off.

4. After two decades of growth, the $10 billion fast-food hamburger business is slowing down. Per capita consumption is only ten percent higher than it was in 1971.
( ) ( ) ( ) ( )

5. Toyota Motor Corp., Japan's no. 1 automaker, announced in 1982 that it was offering a new fiber-reinforcement metal called "ceramic fiber alloy" for use in the manufacture of parts for diesel engines. Despite its claims for increased engine output and higher fuel efficiency, demand for medium to low-priced cars with diesel engines in the U.S. remains very low and very little demand for the new alloy has resulted.
( ) ( ) ( ) ( )

6. One of the most successful products introduced in the last ten years has been videocassettes. As of 1982, over 7,500 outlets sold or rented cassettes. In 1981, cassette distributors purchased about 5.5 million cassettes. This grew to 6.5 million the following year.
( ) ( ) ( ) ( )

7. Package manufacturers are studying the marketing of fresh milk in asceptive packages by Dairyman, Inc. Asceptive packages are new foil-lined paperboard cartons that do not have to be refrigerated. Sales of the new package are slow.
( ) ( ) ( ) ( )

8. Lic Data Corp., manufactures desktop computer display terminals that compete with IBM but also plug into IBM computers. The terminal industry had sales of $750 million in 1982 and $1 billion was forecast for the mid-1980s. Lic's revenue was $13.7 million in 1982 and $40 million in 1983.
( ) ( ) ( ) ( )

NAME *Joseph Lopes*

Exercise 17-3

PRODUCT LIFE CYCLE

The typical product or service is thought to move through an S-shaped sales curve from its introduction to its removal from the market. The four distinct stages in this movement are 1) introduction, 2) growth, 3) maturity, and 4) decline. The <u>introduction</u> stage is a period of slow sales growth, as it takes time for customers to learn about the product's availability and features. Production and marketing costs are high relative to the small number of sales because of the lack of mass-production economies. If the product survives the first stage by gaining market acceptance, it moves into the growth stage. In the <u>growth</u> stage, sales grow substantially and many companies enter the market. Promotion switches from emphasizing primary demand to a focus on selective demand stimulation. In the <u>maturity</u> stage, industry sales level off. Many managers compete in this stage through target market modification, product modification, or marketing mix modification. A substantial and permanent drop in the sales marks the <u>decline</u> stage. If any promotion is done, it is highly selective.

The product life cycle can be applied to a product class (toothpaste), product form (liquid toothpaste drops), or a brand (Pepsodent).

Instructions: Read each of the following statements and indicate which stage is primarily involved.

	Intro-duction	Growth	Matu-rity	De-cline
1. Sales of services utilizing video-taping cameras and portable video-cassette recorders are growing at an increasing rate. One increasingly popular activity is videotaping executives at company golfing outings and preparing short tapes for replays at annual company banquets.	( )	(✓)	( )	( )
2. The Minolta Corp. has recently introduced its Hi-matic AF 2.M, dubbed a "foolproof" camera. Its infrared system focuses automatically, even in total darkness, and it "talks" users out of taking bad pictures by beeping warnings that a flash is needed or that the subject is too close. It is priced at $245.50, and consumers appear to be satisfied with existing alternative choices.	(✓)	( )	( )	( )
3. CCS Communications Control, Inc., an international distributor of protection and security devices, marketed	( )	( )	( )	( )

© 1986 by Prentice-Hall, A Division of Simon & Schuster, Inc. Englewood Cliffs, N.J. 07632. All rights reserved. Printed in the United States of America.

	Intro-duction	Growth	Matu-rity	De-cline

in 1982 a Personal Privacy Protector—a pocket-sized, portable detector of electronic "bugs" for personal use in one's home or office. Sales remain slow.

4. The Hanes Hosiery Division of Consolidated Foods achieved a successful level of pantyhose sales in a stable industry. Seeking opportunities to maintain market share, Hanes marketed pantyhose in unique packages through supermarkets and convenience stores.

( )	( )	(✓)	( )

5. Facing a future decline in sales because of the expected reduction in high-school-aged prospects, Josten, Inc., holder of 40% of the market for class rings and yearbooks, modified its target. It is now advertising in the Wall Street Journal to successful business people that it will duplicate lost school or college class rings.

( )	( )	( )	( )

6. In the mid 1970s the Polaroid Corp. introduced an instant movie system marketed as Polavision. Initial buyer interest in the product was low, although some sales were made. Polaroid continued to produce the camera and viewer until 1979, when it wrote off the $68.5 million Polavision inventory. Sales had dropped to near zero because of more attractive picture-taking alternatives such as videotaping.

( )	( )	( )	( )

7. Because of the decline in birth rates in the 1960s, there are fewer young people of college age today. Faced also with the effects of inflation and students' wanting more emphasis on career preparation, many private prep schools and colleges have had to retrench.

( )	( )	(✓)	( )

8. Just three months after introducing its new line of premium frozen dinners, Le Menu, Campbell Soup Co. raised its projections of annual sales from $75 million to over $100 million. Consumer reaction has been so strong that the company is unable to meet the demand.

( )	( )	( )	( )

NAME _Joseph Lopez_

Exercise 18-1

QUANTITATIVE ANALYSIS: PRICE
ELASTICITY CASE PROBLEM--Wyant
Rent-a-Car

Problem

Wyant Rent-a-Car is a nationwide rental-car company (200 offices).
The company was started in 1962. Wyant's marketing strategy is to offer a
convenient off-airport rental concession at lower prices than the "big three."
For the past fifteen years, the big three companies have monopolized the
"repeat business" (i.e., large companies' traveling salespeople and management).
Wyant's fleet in Chicago has 100 types of cars. With this fleet size, they
must achieve a 65% utility to break even. The office is turning a 75%
utility during the week (Monday through Friday), and achieving their primary goal of getting "repeat business." The problem lies in the fact that
traveling salespeople go home Friday, and for this reason Wyant's utility
figures drop to 25% over the weekend. This low demand for rental cars
during weekends is costing the firm a sizable amount of money.

At this point, management began to consider ways of stimulating demand
for the weekends. The manager, Mr. Jackson, felt that the two main sources
of weekend business were tourists and local residents who needed a new or
extra car during the weekend. Mr. Jackson also felt that demand for this
segment is price elastic. For these reasons, management felt that a special
weekend rate would be profitable. These discount rates would lower average
income per rental, but an increased demand would raise overall weekend
profit.

In computing profit alternatives for the weekend business, Mr. Jackson
has compiled the following financial information:

Weekend depreciation fixed costs	$1,000
Weekend salaries	$ 500
Service cost per car used	$ 5

The renters pay for the gasoline.

The present number of automobiles leased on the weekends is 25, and the
Price revenue per car is $50. Mr. Jackson is considering lowering the revenue
price per car to $35 and thinks the number of automobiles leased will
rise to 50.

© 1986 by Prentice-Hall, A Division of Simon & Schuster, Inc.
Englewood Cliffs, N.J. 07632. All rights reserved.
Printed in the United States of America.

Basic Concepts to Apply

Contribution = Sales - Variable Costs

Net Profit = Contribution - Fixed Costs

$$\text{Break Even Point} = \frac{\text{Fixed Costs}}{\text{Unit Sales Price - Unit Variable Costs}}$$

Fixed Costs: The cost is fixed if it remains constant over a relevant range even when the volume of activity varies.

Variable Costs: The cost is variable if it changes when the volume of activity changes.

1. Compute sales, contribution, and net profit when cars are leased for $50 on weekends.

Sales $1250.

Contribution $$1250, - 250

Net Profit (~~~~~~) $1125 — 1500 = (-375)

2. Compute sales, contribution, and net profit when cars are leased for $35 on weekends.

Sales $1750,

Contribution 1750, - 250 = 1500

Net Profit 1500 - 1500 = ∅

Exercise 18-2

QUANTITATIVE ANALYSIS: INCREMENTAL DEMAND CASE PROBELM--Regency Beer Company

Problem

The Regency Beer Company is a regional beer manufacturer located in Dallas. The beer is presently distributed in Texas, Oklahoma, New Mexico, Kansas, Arkansas, and Louisiana. The company comptroller indicated the following financial situation in 1985:

Regency case sales	$5,000,000
Price per case to wholesalers	$6.00
Recommended price per case to retailers	$7.25
Recommended price per case to customers	$8.75

Costs

Plant overhead	$4,000,000
Marketing overhead	1,000,000
General Administration	2,000,000
Advertising	5,000,000
Production cost per case	$2.00
Distribution and selling cost per case	$1.00

Regency is presently operating at 65% of production capacity. Regency's share of market in 1985 in its markets has declined from 21% in 1970 to 15% in 1985. Major competitors in 1985 were:

Budweiser -- 32% share of market

Miller -- 21% share of market

Coors -- 18% share of market

© 1986 by Prentice-Hall, A Division of Simon & Schuster, Inc.
Englewood Cliffs, N.J. 07632. All rights reserved.
Printed in the United States of America.

<u>Basic Concepts to Apply</u>

$$\text{Contribution} = \text{Sales} - \text{Variable Costs}$$

$$\text{Net Profit} = \text{Contribution} - \text{Fixed Costs}$$

$$\text{Break Even Point} = \frac{\text{Fixed Costs}}{\text{Unit Sales Price} - \text{Unit Variable Costs}}$$

Fixed Costs: The cost is fixed if it remains constant over a relevant range even when the volume of activity varies.

Variable Costs: The cost is variable if it changes when the volume of activity changes.

1. What was Regency's net profit in 1985?

_____

2. What was the break-even point in case sales for 1985?

_____

The Bigboy retail liquor distributor in New York was interested in buying 500,000 cases of Regency beer if the price was low enough. The marketing manager estimated that the 500,000 cases could be shipped directly to New York for $50,000 in addition to the regular distribution and selling cost. Regency decided to sell 500,000 cases to the Bigboy retail liquor distributor at $4.00 per case.

3. How much additional contribution will Regency make by selling the beer to Bigboy?

_____

Exercise 18-3   QUANTITATIVE ANALYSIS: BREAK-EVEN
                                 CASE PROBLEM--Silver Airline

Problem

Silver Airline is a regional airline that operates flights from Midway Airport in Chicago to Milwaukee. The following financial situation existed in 1985:

Number of regular tickets sold	100,000
Number of discount tickets sold	50,000
Price for regular ticket	$30
Price for discount ticket	$20

Costs

Equipment and maintenance	$1,000,000
Personnel equipment overhead	1,000,000
General management	500,000
Advertising	500,000
Direct cost per passenger	$5

Basic Concepts to Apply

Contribution = Sales - Variable Costs

Net Profit = Contribution - Fixed Costs

$$\text{Break Even Point} = \frac{\text{Fixed Costs}}{\text{Unit Sales Price - Unit Variable Costs}}$$

Fixed Costs: The cost is fixed if it remains constant over a relevant range even when the volume of activity varies.

Variable Costs: The cost is variable if it changes when the volume of activity changes.

© 1986 by Prentice-Hall, A Division of Simon & Schuster, Inc.
Englewood Cliffs, N.J. 07632. All rights reserved.
Printed in the United States of America.

Silver is presently operating at 68% of plane capacity.

1. Compute sales, contribution, and net profit for 1985.

Sales _____

Contribution _____

Net Profit _____

2. Golden's major competitor decided to lower its regular fare from $30 to $20. If Golden lowered its regular fare from $30 to $20 without changing the number of tickets sold, compute sales, contribution, and net profit for 1985.

Sales _____

Contribution _____

Net Profit _____

3. How many tickets priced at $20 would Golden have to sell to break even in 1985?

Break-Even Point _____

NAME _____

Exercise 18-4

QUANTITATIVE ANALYSIS: ELASTICITY
AND BREAKEVEN CASE PROBLEM--
Leisure-Life Products Company

Problem

Mr. Ted Bates formed the Leisure-Life Products Company to manufacture
and market a line of wooden hot tubs complete with heaters, plumbing, and
water jets. He had first observed the popularity of hot tubs in California
when he visited there on a business trip. He returned home convinced that
he could make a great deal of money manufacturing and selling a similar
product in his home state. After designing and testing a working model of
the hot tub, Mr. Bates estimated the following costs for the first year of
operation:

Costs

Manufacturing overhead	$50,000
Marketing and general overhead	50,000
Direct manufacturing cost per hot tub	200
Direct marketing and distribution cost per hot tub	100

In determining his selling price to the potential customers, Mr. Bates
felt that there were a number of prospects in his home territory who had
heard about hot tubs, had high disposable incomes, and would be glad to pay
a premium price for the hot tubs. He estimated that if he set a sales
price of $1,000 per tub, he could sell 250 hot tubs the first year.

His tennis partner, with whom he discussed his plans, indicated that a
mass market might exist if Mr. Bates lowered the selling price. By lowering
the price, Mr. Bates also felt that potential competitors might be dis-
couraged from entering the market to manufacture hot tubs. He estimated
that he could sell 500 hot tubs the first year if he set a sales price of
$600 per hot tub.

1. What would the first-year profit be with a sales price of $1,000?

_____

© 1986 by Prentice-Hall, A Division of Simon & Schuster, Inc.
Englewood Cliffs, N.J. 07632. All rights reserved.
Printed in the United States of America.

2. What would the first-year profit be with a sales price of $600?

_____

Basic Concepts to Apply

$$\text{Contribution} = \text{Sales} - \text{Variable Costs}$$

$$\text{Net Profit} = \text{Contribution} - \text{Fixed Costs}$$

$$\text{Break Even Point} = \frac{\text{Fixed Costs}}{\text{Unit Sales Price} - \text{Unit Variable Costs}}$$

Fixed Costs: The cost is fixed if it remains constant over a relevant range even when the volume of activity varies.

Variable Costs: The cost is variable if it changes when the volume of activity changes.

3. What is the break-even point in number of tubs sold with a sales price of $1,000?

_____

4. What is the break-even point in number of tubs sold with a sales price of $600?

_____

NAME _____

Exercise 18-5   QUANTITATIVE ANALYSIS: PRICING CASE
                                     PROBLEM--Vestal Products, Inc.

Problem

    Vestal Products, Inc., manufactures a wide line of electrical products,
such as outlets, caps, switches, fuse holders, cable, and conduit. These
products were sold to electrical-supply wholesalers by manufacturers' agents.
The wholesalers in turn generally sold to electrical contractors. Vestal
Products, Inc., quoted list prices that permitted contractors to allow final
users 25 percent off list and that permitted wholesalers to allow contractors 40 percent off list. The company gave wholesalers 40 percent and 10
percent off list. Accordingly, the wholesalers would get a gross margin of
10 percent of the suggested price to contractors. The compensation of the
selling agents was set at 10 percent of the company's selling price to
wholesalers.

    Assuming that Vestal Products, Inc., sells $1,000/month of product at
list prices, in dollar amounts:

1. How much does the final user pay?

        _____

2. How much does the contractor pay?

        _____

3. How much does the wholesaler pay?

        _____

4. How much does the manufacturer's agent receive?

        _____

5. What are the actual dollar sales of Vestal Products, Inc., on this
    transaction?

        _____

© 1986 by Prentice-Hall, A Division of Simon & Schuster, Inc.
Englewood Cliffs, N.J. 07632. All rights reserved.
Printed in the United States of America.

Exercise 18-6

QUANTITATIVE ANALYSIS: FIXED AND
VARIABLE COSTS--Harris Company

Problem

The Harris Company has the following costs:

Manufacturing Overhead	$30,000
Distribution Overhead	20,000
Manufacturing costs per unit	700
Distribution costs per unit	300

Compute the following table:

Cost	Quantity Produced				
	0	1	2	3	4
Total costs					
Total Fixed Costs					
Total Variable Costs					
Average Costs per unit					
Average Fixed cost per unit					
Average variable cost per unit					

Exercise 19-1   GENERAL PRICING APPROACHES

Three pricing approaches that firms use in setting price are 1) cost-based, 2) buyer-based, and 3) competition-based. <u>Cost-based pricing</u> is determined by the firm on the basis of all of its cost, including allocation of overhead. Cost-based pricing includes markup pricing, cost-plus pricing, and target profit pricing. Markup pricing is frequently used at the retail level, where the retailer adds different markups to various goods. Cost-plus pricing is used for nonroutine jobs, such as construction and engineering. Target profit pricing is used by capital-intensive firms and utilities, where a price is determined that will give the firm a target rate of return based upon costs and a standard volume. <u>Buyer-based pricing</u> is based upon customer perceptions and demand elasticities. Perceived-value pricing is based upon value as perceived by the buyer and is based upon different market segments having varying elasticities of demand. <u>Competition-based pricing</u> is based upon the actual or estimated pricing of competitors and includes going-rate pricing and competitive bidding. Going-rate pricing is the firm's pricing its product at the same level as its competitors. Competitive bidding is used when two or more firms independently submit bids for specific projects. Competitive price wars occur occasionally, but are usually of short duration.

Instructions: Read each of the following statements and indicate which approach applies.

	Cost-Based Pricing	Buyer-Based Pricing	Competition-Based Pricing
1. Owners of Citibank savings accounts in New York City have to keep at least $500 in their account to avoid a $1.50/ per month charge. Customers who open checking accounts as well as savings accounts are not charged a fee. Some banks require higher minimum balances for single savings accounts while others charge less.	( )	( )	( )
2. In 1984, the final year of a five-year Japanese restriction of car exports to the United States, the head of the American International Automobile Dealers Association said, "It's rare to find a [Japanese and West European] dealership these days that isn't making a $3,000 to $3,500 net profit per car."	( )	( )	( )
3. To help meet off-price apparel chain prices, department stores are taking	( )	( )	( )

© 1986 by Prentice-Hall, A Division of Simon & Schuster, Inc.
Englewood Cliffs, N.J. 07632. All rights reserved.
Printed in the United States of America.   121

	Cost-Based Pricing	Buyer-Based Pricing	Competition-Based Pricing

more frequent markdowns.

		Cost-Based Pricing	Buyer-Based Pricing	Competition-Based Pricing
4.	After four years on top of the color TV market, Zenith watched RCA cut into its market share. Zenith broadly slashed prices and increased its market share of color TV sales.	( )	( )	( )
5.	When home permanents were first introduced to women at twenty-five cents a package, women were not interested in the product. After the same home permanents were repackaged and sold for $1.25 a package, they were a great success.	( )	( )	( )
6.	At many hospitals throughout the United States, the cost of operating a hospital has risen so much that the price of a semiprivate room has increased to over $300 per day.	( )	( )	( )
7.	Most movie theatre tickets are priced cheaper during the day than at night.	( )	( )	( )
8.	The average markup for books sold in many department stores has been 34 percent during the last couple of years.	( )	( )	( )
9.	In 1976, one of the longest and most costly price wars in supermarket history occurred in Chicago. Jewel and Dominick supermarkets reduced food prices on thousands of items.	( )	( )	( )
10.	Because of consumer acceptance, Smuckers, which manufactures jellies and preserves, is able to price its products higher than competitors' products. Smuckers' slogan is, "If it's Smuckers, it's got to be good."	( )	( )	( )
11.	In the automobile tire industry, Goodyear generally sets its prices for replacement tires so that it matches its competitors. Its objectives are to maintain market share and to have price stability.	( )	( )	( )

NAME *Joseph Lopez*

Exercise 19-2   GENERAL PRICING APPROACHES

Three pricing approaches that firms use in setting price are 1) cost-based, 2) buyer-based, and 3) competition-based. <u>Cost-based pricing</u> is determined by the firm on the basis of all of its cost, including allocation of overhead. Cost-based pricing includes markup pricing, cost-plus pricing, and target profit pricing. Markup pricing is frequently used at the retail level, where the retailer adds different markups to various goods. Cost-plus pricing is used for nonroutine jobs, such as construction and engineering. Target profit pricing is used by capital-intensive firms and utilities, where a price is determined that will give the firm a target rate of return based on costs and a standard volume. <u>Buyer-based pricing</u> is based upon customer perceptions and demand elasticities. Perceived-value pricing is based upon value as perceived by the buyer and is based upon different market segments having varying elasticities of demand. <u>Competition-based pricing</u> is based upon the actual or estimated pricing of competitors and includes going-rate pricing and competitive bidding. Going-rate pricing is the firm's pricing its product at the same level as its competitors. Competitive bidding is used when two or more firms independently submit bids for specific projects. Competitive price wars occur occasionally, but are usually of short duration.

Instructions: Read each of the following statements and indicate which approach applies.

	Cost-Based Pricing	Buyer-Based Pricing	Competition-Based Pricing
1. Foley's department store was able to offer lower sheet prices by eliminating a textile manufacturer's funding of Foley's advertising of its semi-annual white sale.	(✓)	( )	( )
2. Patents are about to expire on some of the most commonly used medicines, including the best-selling tranquilizer, Valium.	( )	( )	( )
3. A manufacturer of scarves prices its product so that they are sold at retail in three different price categories. $5 scarves are sold to the economy-minded segment; $8-10 scarves are sold to customers who want medium-quality scarves; and $16 scarves are the top-of-the-line scarves sold to the quality-minded segment.	( )	( )	( )
4. Observing designer Henry Grethel's	( )	( )	( )

© 1986 by Prentice-Hall, A Division of Simon & Schuster, Inc.
Englewood Cliffs, N.J. 07632. All rights reserved.
Printed in the United States of America.

123

	Cost-Based Pricing	Buyer-Based Pricing	Competition-Based Pricing

label at off-price stores, the upscale specialty store Sakowitz dropped that line and replaced it with private label merchandise.

No.		Cost-Based Pricing	Buyer-Based Pricing	Competition-Based Pricing
5.	Many electrical utility companies have an automatic increase in their price of electrical power based on increases in the cost of fuel and other raw materials.	( )	( )	( )
6.	Many marketing-research firms price their services using the concept of billable hours. Billable hours are determined on the basis of cost, plus some profit margin.	( )	( )	( )
7.	Financial advisor Howard Ruff publishes a semimonthly newsletter, Ruff Times, and charges subscribers $125 a year. Ruff contends that people will pay that price if the newsletter is good.	( )	(✓)	( )
8.	Retail stores now sell eyeglasses that are designed by such well-known fashion experts as Ralph Lauren and Bill Blass. These premium-priced glasses are targeted to the upper level of society.	( )	( )	( )
9.	In 1977, American Airlines cut the regular New York-Los Angeles round-trip fare from $415 to $227. Within a week, United and TWA matched the $227 price.	( )	( )	( )
10.	Macy's and Gimbel's department stores in New York City have engaged in vicious but short price wars, where neither retail chain would knowingly be undersold.	( )	( )	(✓)
11.	Armco Steel Company in Houston reduced its prices of steel sold to the oil industry. This action was necessary due to cheaper Japanese steel being imported to the port of Houston.	( )	( )	( )
12.	The University of Illinois bookstore has a 20% markup pricing policy for all new college textbooks sold in the bookstore.	( )	( )	( )

Exercise 19-3   GENERAL PRICING APPROACHES

Three pricing approaches that firms use in setting price are 1) cost-based, 2) buyer-based, and 3) competition-based. Cost-based pricing is determined by the firm on the basis of all of its cost, including allocation of overhead. Cost-based pricing includes markup pricing, cost-plus pricing, and target profit pricing. Markup pricing is frequently used at the retail level, where the retailer adds different markups to various goods. Cost-plus-pricing is used for nonroutine jobs, such as construction and engineering. Target profit pricing is used by capital-intensive firms and utilities, where a price is determined that will give the firm a target rate of return based upon costs and a standard volume. Buyer-based pricing is based upon customer perceptions and demand elasticities. Perceived-value pricing is based upon value as perceived by the buyer and is based upon different market segments having varying elasticities of demand. Competition-based pricing is based upon the actual or estimated pricing of competitors and include going-rate pricing and competitive bidding. Going-rate pricing is the firm's pricing its product at the same level as its competitors. Competitive bidding is used when two or more firms independently submit bids for specific projects. Competitive price wars occur occasionally, but are usually of short duration.

Instructions: Read each of the following statements and indicate which approach applies.

	Cost-Based Pricing	Buyer-Based Pricing	Competition-Based Pricing
1. By traveling on short notice, members of Vacations To Go have their choice of over 100 vacation trips at reduced rates. Tour operators who have unsold seats make them available to VTG at discount prices shortly before departure time.	( )	( )	( )
2. By pricing below costs, Wilson Supply Company was able to get a foot in the door and prove to a large customer that it was capable of meeting delivery needs.	( )	( )	( )
3. TWA initiated three classes of service on domestic flights in 1982. In the "ambassador class," this highest priced service featured free drinks and china dishware. Travelers in "businessmen class" paid $10 to $30 more than the regular "coach fare," so that they could travel better.	( )	( )	( )

© 1986 by Prentice-Hall, A Division of Simon & Schuster, Inc.
Englewood Cliffs, N.J. 07632. All rights reserved.
Printed in the United States of America.

	Cost-Based Pricing	Buyer-Based Pricing	Competition-Based Pricing
4. Curtis-Mathes has elected to set a high price for its TV sets. Its advertising slogan is, "Curtis-Mathes is the highest-priced television set in America, and it's darn well worth it."	( )	( )	( )
5. Northrup Corporation has contracted with the Department of Defense (DOD) to develop a secret weapon system. Because of the advance technology required, the contract allows Northrup to recover its actual cost plus a reasonable profit margin.	( )	( )	( )
6. Marijuana growers of Northern Carolina are reported to believe that Peruvian seabird fertilizer is the Rolls Royce of fertilizer. It sells for four times its value, according to the fertilizer industry.	( )	( )	( )
7. Lobel's is a neighborhood butcher store in New York City that sells meats and poultry to such luminaries as Robert Redford and Jacqueline Onassis. Lobel's charges $14.89 for a pound of veal scallops, even though A&P, a few doors away, charges only $6.20 a pound.	( )	( )	( )
8. Retail service stations frequently engage in gasoline price wars with other retail service stations in the same neighborhood.	( )	( )	( )
9. In 1982, General Motors offered cash rebates of up to $2000 on some of its automobiles. The rebate offer from GM occurred after Chrysler started offering cash rebates.	( )	( )	( )
10. GM determines its prices for its line of automobiles based upon an ideal rate of return, relevant costs, and an estimated volume of sales each year.	( )	( )	( )

Exercise 20-1   NEW PRODUCT PRICING STRATEGIES

Two major new-product pricing strategies are 1) market penetration pricing and 2) market skimming pricing. <u>Market-penetration pricing</u> occurs when the firm establishes a low price in an attempt to gain a large or dominant share of the market and achieve production economies. This strategy is appropriate in discouraging potential competitors from entering the market. When the market is estimated to be price-elastic and large-volume sales are expected, market-penetration pricing seems to be a good strategy. <u>Market-skimming pricing</u> occurs when the firm sets a high price for its new product. The high price helps the firm recover its research and development costs quickly and supports the image of a superior product. In the absence of a patent, this skimming strategy may attract competition to the marketplace.

> Instructions: Read each of the following state-
> ments and indicate which strategy has been
> selected.

	Market Penetration	Market Skimming
1. J. Brannam, a subsidiary of Woolworth's, which opened in 1979, is operating as an off-price retailer. Prices are 20-50% lower than at department stores and specialty shops.	( )	( )
2. La Quinta Motor Inns,Inc., provides its guests with clean and comfortable rooms. The room rates are about 20% less than those of comparable motor inns.	( )	( )
3. Alberto-Culver introduced Alberto-Balsam hair shampoo at $1.49. Wella Balsam, the major competitor to Alberto-Culver, was selling its hair shampoo for $1.98 at the time of the Alberto-Culver introduction.	( )	( )
4. Mercedes-Benz prices its automobile much higher than other automobiles. Most owners of Mercedes-Benz think the quality of the car justifies the price.	( )	( )
5. Hewlett-Packard Company offered high-priced pocket calculators to select segments of the market. H-P continually	( )	( )

© 1986 by Prentice-Hall, A Division of Simon & Schuster, Inc.
Englewood Cliffs, N.J. 07632. All rights reserved.
Printed in the United States of America.

varies its product line to justify its higher price.

6. Polaroid introduced its Polaroid SX-70 camera using a high initial price, which helped defray the large research and development costs. With a patent on its camera, Polaroid was able to protect itself from competitors.   ( )   ( )

7. The 7-11 retail stores have pioneered the convenience store concept. Their pricing strategy has been to sell most of their products at higher prices than supermarkets.   ( )   ( )

8. Charles Schwab has positioned his firm as a discount brokerage. Schwab prices his commission for buying and selling stocks much lower than brokerage firms like Merrill Lynch.   ( )   ( )

9. Nike, Inc., primarily a marketer of specialty sports shoes also sells athletic apparel. Its suppliers of apparel include the Russell Corp., the nation's largest producer. Nike offers its branded apparel at significantly higher prices than Russell, thus avoiding competition with its supplier.   ( )   ( )

10. Movie studios had typically priced video-cassettes as high as $79.95. Columbia sold only 100,000 units of Tootsie grossing $5 million but Paramount sold Raiders of the Lost Ark at $39.95 and sold one million units or $40 million at retail.   ( )   ( )

11. After experiencing a 4.5% industry drop in cigarette sales, R. J. Reynolds switched its Doral brand to the discount category.   ( )   ( )

12. Although diesel fuel costs less than gasoline to produce, major oil companies raised diesel prices above premium gasoline prices in 1984.   ( )   ( )

Exercise 20-2   NEW PRODUCT PRICING STRATEGIES

    Two major new-product pricing strategies are 1) market-penetration pricing and 2) market-skimming pricing. <u>Market-penetration pricing</u> occurs when the firm establishes a low price in an attempt to gain a large or dominant share of the market and achieve production economies. This strategy is appropriate in discouraging potential competitors from entering the market. When the market is estimated to be price-elastic, and large-volume sales are expected, market-penetration pricing seems to be a good strategy. <u>Market-skimming pricing</u> occurs when the firm sets a high price for its new product. The high price helps the firm recover its research and development costs quickly and supports the image of a superior product. In the absence of a patent, this skimming strategy may attract competition to the marketplace.

> Instructions: Read each of the following state-
> ments and indicate which strategy has been
> selected.

	Market Penetration	Market Skimming
1. The Broadmoor is a resort hotel in Colorado that has a 5-star Mobil rating. The Broadmoor room rates are very high, and they cater to very wealthy people.	( )	( )
2. Curtis-Mathes manufactures and markets a quality line of television sets. In its advertisements, Curtis-Mathes explicitly states that its TV sets are the most expensive on the market.	( )	( )
3. Dow Chemical Company stresses low-margin commodity chemical products. It prices its products low to build up a dominant market share.	( )	( )
4. MCI Communications introduced its long-distance phone service as a major competitor to American Telephone and Telegraph. MCI priced its service below AT&T's long-distance rates.	( )	( )
5. When Southwest Airlines began business, its major competitors were Braniff and Texas International. Southwest priced a ticket from Dallas to Houston at $20, instead of the existing $27 price	( )	( )

© 1986 by Prentice-Hall, A Division of Simon & Schuster, Inc.
Englewood Cliffs, N.J. 07632. All rights reserved.
Printed in the United States of America.

charged by competitors.

6. The Concorde was the first super-
sonic plane in the world used in
commercial flights. The original ticket
price to travel from London to New York
was much higher than those of competing
flights.

( )　　( )

7. Xerox for years has charged a high price
for its equipment, paper, and service.
Having patents on its equipment, Xerox
has limited competition.

( )　　( )

8. Bristol-Myers introduced Datril as a non-
aspirin acetaminophen to compete with
Tylenol. Datril was deliberately priced
lower than Tylenol.

( )　　( )

9. Although there was a shortage of gypsum
wallboard when the housing recovery began
in 1985, prices were not expected to rise
because gypsum producers felt a big rise
in price could stimulate more capacity
either by encouraging some domestic producers to reopen closed plants or at-
tracting supplies from abroad.

( )　　( )

10. Noting that only 12,292 cars were sold by
his firm in 1909 when the price of his
touring car was $950, Henry Ford reduced
his price and by 1916 sold 577,036 cars
at $360. Evaluate his second strategy.

( )　　( )

11. Conair Corp., highly successful in selling hair dryers to the 25-and-under market, introduced in 1985 High Energy, a
line of $10 slimline phones in "hot
fashion colors."

( )　　( )

12. Vehicle Radar Safety Systems, a private
firm, attempted to introduce Rashid Radar
Safety Brake, a radar unit that detects
obstacles and alerts drivers. To obtain
distributors attractive margins were offered. The system will retail at $558.

( )　　( )

13. Wine distributor Vin-Ordinaire, featuring
a "plain brown label," ships 3000-5000
cases a month of its Cheap Red Wine
and Cheap White Wine. Both are moderately
priced from $2.50 to $2.99 per fifth.

( )　　( )

Exercise 20-3   NEW-PRODUCT PRICING STRATEGIES

Two major new-product pricing strategies are 1) market-penetration pricing and 2) market-skimming pricing. <u>Market-penetration pricing</u> occurs when the firm establishes a low price in an attempt to gain a large or dominant share of the market and achieve production economies. This strategy is appropriate in discouraging potential competitors from entering the market. When the market is estimated to be price-elastic and large-volume sales are expected, market-penetration pricing seems to be a good strategy. <u>Market-skimming pricing</u> occurs when the firm sets a high price for its new product. The high price helps the firm recover its research and development costs quickly and supports the image of a superior product. In the absence of a patent, this skimming strategy may attract competition to the marketplace.

Instructions: Read each of the following statements and indicate which strategy has been selected.

		Market Penetration	Market Skimming
1.	H&R Block sells an income-tax service to clients. Its service is much less expensive than professional accounting firms.	(✓)	( )
2.	Chivas Regal scotch whisky is priced higher than most scotch whisky. Buyers state that Chivas Regal is top quality.	( )	( )
3.	Texas Instruments introduced a new digital watch in 1976 for $20. In 1974-75, the lowest-priced digital watch had been selling for $125.	( )	(✓)
4.	When Bic entered the disposable pen market which was dominated by Write Brothers and Lindy, Bic priced its new pen at 19 cents. This price was substantially lower than prices of competitors.	( )	( )
5.	Over a number of years, IBM has introduced its new computers at a high price. This allowed IBM to recover its R&D costs quickly.	( )	( )
6.	DuPont introduced Quiana, a synthetic fabric with the feel of silk, to the high-fashion market. DuPont sold	( )	(✓)

© 1986 by Prentice-Hall, A Division of Simon & Schuster, Inc.
Englewood Cliffs, N.J. 07632. All rights reserved.
Printed in the United States of America.

	Market Penetration	Market Skimming
Quiana at a high initial price.		
7. Sara Lee has manufactured and sold a high-quality line of frozen cakes for years. Sara Lee has priced its products consistently higher than its competitors'.	( )	( )
8. Roundy's, a Milwaukee food wholesaler, owns Pick 'n Save warehouse food stores. Operating with few frills, Pick 'n Save prices its food 15% less than regular supermarkets.	( )	( )
9. One recent graduate estimated that obtaining his undergraduate degree from Harvard cost his family $50,716.	( )	(✓)
10. With 270 lawyers in 117 offices across the U.S. and plans for 400 to 500 offices within five years, Hyatt Legal Services is the biggest legal-clinic chain. Prices are kept low by concentrating on simple legal work.	( )	( )
11. When personal radio pagers, or "beepers", were introduced, the initial price ranged from $150 to $200 in 1976. Within a year the market tripled. Some beepers now sell for $50.	( )	( )
12. Warner Home Video, the Warner Communications, Inc., home-video unit, initially planned to sell videocassette tapes of the movie Risky Business at $79.95 but the producer insisted the price be $39.95. He wanted the price low so that "kids could afford to buy it."	( )	( )
13. In 1984 and 1985 the strength of the American dollar led many importers to expect lower foreign prices. Burberry's, famous British manufacturer of trench coats, seemed to be following a strategy of "take it while you can."	( )	( )

Exercise 21-1   PRICE DISCOUNTS

   Price discounts are reductions from list prices that are granted by a
seller to a buyer. There are four major types of price discounts. They
are 1) quantity discounts, 2) cash discounts, 3) functional discounts, and
4) seasonal discounts. Quantity discounts are given to the buyer who purchases in larger quantities. This discount is based on cost savings in
production, transportation or storage. Cash discounts are given to the
buyer for prompt payment of the bill or for cash purchases. Functional
discounts (trade discounts) are compensation for performing marketing
functions required by the seller. This discount is a price reduction
given to channel members, usually wholesalers and retailers.
Seasonal discounts are given to buyers for buying out of season
or at the end of the season.

   Instructions: Read each of the following statements
   and indicate which type of discount applies.

	Quantity Discounts	Cash Discounts	Functional Discounts	Seasonal Discounts
1. Travel and hotel prices in Cancun, Mexico, are drastically reduced during the summer as compared to the winter months.	( )	( )	( )	( )
2. With almost two hundred hospitals that it either owns or manages, Hospital Corporation of America is the world's largest owner-manager of hospitals. Taking advantage of its economy of scale, HCA buys Band-Aids much cheaper by the box-car than by the box.	( )	( )	( )	( )
3. Prentice-Hall gives twenty percent off of suggested retail list prices to bookstores selling textbooks to college students.	( )	( )	( )	( )
4. Most purchasing managers in large industrial firms make sure that the terms of contract include a two per-cent discount for payment of the purchase within a reasonable time period.	( )	( )	( )	( )
5. Virtually all retail department stores severely reduce their prices	( )	( )	( )	( )

© 1986 by Prentice-Hall, A Division of Simon & Schuster, Inc.
Englewood Cliffs, N.J. 07632. All rights reserved.
Printed in the United States of America.

	Quantity Discounts	Cash Discounts	Functional Discounts	Seasonal Discounts

on clothing immediately following
Christmas.

6. McDonald Corporation buys paper products used in its franchised retail outlets in very large volume. Because of this volume, McDonald's receives a cheaper price for the paper products. ( ) ( ) ( ) ( )

7. Customers at Exxon retail service stations are charged four cents less per gallon if they pay cash instead of charging the purchase on a credit card. ( ) ( ) ( ) ( )

8. Industrial distributors are independent middlemen who buy, store, and sell industrial products to industrial users. Many industrial distributors receive a 30 to 40% discount off the price paid by the users. ( ) ( ) ( ) ( )

9. Wishing to expand his firm in other directions, the president of Gulf & Western Industries, Inc., sold the firm's consumer and industrial products group to Wickes Cos. at an attractive price. ( ) ( ) ( ) ( )

10. Avis announced that travellers who have rented a car in Miami for five days were entitled to two additional days without charge. ( ) ( ) ( ) ( )

11. Versailles, Inc., developers of a 331 beachfront condominium, offered a $1000 discount on its final 50 units if buyers purchased prior to summer. ( ) ( ) ( ) ( )

12. The Ramada Renaissance Hotel in San Francisco will guarantee a room rate of $95 next year to guests who pay full fare--up to $150 per night--for a room this year. ( ) ( ) ( ) ( )

Exercise 21-2   PRICE DISCOUNTS

Price discounts are reductions from list prices that are granted by a seller to a buyer. There are four major types of price discounts. They are 1) quantity discounts, 2) cash discounts, 3) functional discounts, and 4) seasonal discounts. <u>Quantity discounts</u> are given to the buyer who purchases in larger quantities. This discount is based on cost savings in production, transportation or storage. <u>Cash discounts</u> are given to the buyer for prompt payment of the bill or for cash purchases. <u>Functional discounts</u> (trade discounts) are compensation for performing marketing functions required by the seller. This discount is a price reduction given to channel members, usually wholesalers and retailers. <u>Seasonal discounts</u> are given to buyers for buying out of season or at the end of the season.

Instructions: Read each of the following statements and indicate which type of discount applies.

	Quantity Discounts	Cash Discounts	Functional Discounts	Seasonal Discounts
1. Scripto Pen Corporation manufactures pencils and ballpoint pens. Scripto allows all wholesalers a twenty-five percent markup on the price charged to retailers. Retailers were granted a 35 percent markup on the suggested retail price.	( )	( )	( )	( )
2. Beer wholesalers in a number of territories allow their customers to buy on a thirty-day account and still take a traditional two percent discount.	( )	( )	( )	( )
3. Steak and Ale, a steak chain owned by Pillsbury, buys beef at favorable prices because of its large-volume purchases.	( )	( )	( )	( )
4. Many furniture stores will grant a 10 percent discount to customers for paying cash rather than using some form of credit.	( )	( )	( )	( )
5. Carrier Corporation gives a special discount in October to every retail appliance dealer who places	( )	( )	( )	( )

© 1986 by Prentice-Hall, A Division of Simon & Schuster, Inc.
Englewood Cliffs, N.J. 07632. All rights reserved.
Printed in the United States of America.

	Quantity Discounts	Cash Discounts	Functional Discounts	Seasonal Discounts

an order for air conditioners in the middle of November.

6. To clear out the old models, automobile dealers generally cut the prices of their current automobiles immediately before the introduction of new models in the fall of the year. ( ) ( ) ( ) ( )

7. Manufacturing agents are used in the sale of machinery and equipment, where the manufacturers are not very large. These independent middlemen receive a commission for selling the machinery and equipment to industrial users. ( ) ( ) ( ) ( )

8. Kroger Supermarket receives favorable prices in its purchases of canned fruits and vegetables because of the volume of purchase. ( ) ( ) ( ) ( )

9. Although RCA offered retailers in 1981 margins of 50% on its videodisc player, few retailers responded. In 1984 RCA discontinued the line after reported losses of over $500 million. ( ) ( ) ( ) ( )

10. The Atlanta Journal sells advertising space to retailers at $11.27 per column inch. If retailers buy 100 inches a year the rate is $8.43 and for 10,000 inches it is $7.97. ( ) ( ) ( ) ( )

11. When it entered the Boston-Houston market, Continental Airlines offered a price structure that differed from competitors. The one-way fare flying Monday through Thursday was $170. If one flies off-peak, the one-way fare is $129. ( ) ( ) ( ) ( )

12. Virtually all department stores severely reduce their prices on sports clothes immediately following the Fourth of July. ( ) ( ) ( ) ( )

NAME _____

Exercise 21-3   PRICE DISCOUNTS

Price discounts are reductions from list prices that are granted by a seller to a buyer. There are four major types of price discounts. They are 1) quantity discounts, 2) cash discounts, 3) functional discounts, and 4) seasonal discounts. <u>Quantity discounts</u> are given to the buyer who purchases in larger quantities. This discount is based on cost savings in production, transportation, or storage. <u>Cash discounts</u> are given to the buyer for prompt payment of the bill or for cash purchases. <u>Functional discounts</u> (trade discounts) are compensation for performing marketing functions required by the seller. This discount is a price reduction given to channel members, usually wholesalers and retailers. <u>Seasonal discounts</u> are given to buyers for buying out of season or at the end of the season.

Instructions: Read each of the following statements and indicate which type of discount applies.

	Quantity Discounts	Cash Discounts	Functional Discounts	Seasonal Discounts
1. Toro Corporation gives its retailers a price discount every September, which is passed on to consumers as an incentive to buy a lawn mower in the fall.	( )	( )	( )	( )
2. Saga Corporation, a leader in the food-service industry, has many contract food arrangements for hospitals and universities. With its large size, the corporation takes advantage of volume discounts with most of its food products.	( )	( )	( )	( )
3. Prices for apartments in many college towns are reduced during the summer months because the demand is sharply down from the fall and spring semsters.	( )	( )	( )	( )
4. Record-rack jobbers are given a 50% discount from list prices by all major record manufacturers. The jobbers stock record racks in many retail outlets.	( )	( )	( )	( )
5. Toys R Us buys its toys in such	( )	( )	( )	( )

© 1986 by Prentice-Hall, A Division of Simon & Schuster, Inc.
Englewood Cliffs, N.J. 07632. All rights reserved.
Printed in the United States of America.

	Quantity Discounts	Cash Discounts	Functional Discounts	Seasonal Discounts

volume that it receives a larger discount over the independent retailers, who buy in much smaller quantities.

6. Most electric utilities allow a substantial reduction in their monthly electrical bills if the customer pays within a designated time period.

( )	( )	( )	( )

7. U.S. Pioneer Electronics Corporation is a leader in the manufacture of hi-fi products. It uses about 20 independent sales representatives on commission to sell to its retail dealers.

( )	( )	( )	( )

8. Independent oil jobbers buy gasoline and gasoline-related products from oil producers. The typical credit terms are 2/10, n/30 (two percent discount if paid within 10 days, with the net amount due in 30 days).

( )	( )	( )	( )

9. The Meridian Savings Association, a savings and loan association, located in the Southwest, offered 10.25% interest on depositor's certificates of deposit if the amount exceeded $100,000. If not the rate was 10 %.

( )	( )	( )	( )

10. Camera customers who are willing to forego the services of a salesperson can order the Leica R4-S camera at a discount by mail from a New York City camera store.

( )	( )	( )	( )

11. When Commodore Corp., manufacturers of mobile-homes, feared it would file for bankruptcy, it offered attractive terms to distributors who would pay for homes prior to delivery.

( )	( )	( )	( )

Exercise 22-1

QUANTITATIVE ANALYSIS: DISTRIBUTION
CASE PROBLEMS--Lucore Steel Company

Problem

Lucore Steel is a steel manufacturer with three mini-mills and sales districts in the southern United States. Last year, Lucore earned a 38% return on equity. The company uses scrap steel as a raw material and limits its products to simple bars and angles for local markets. Mini-mills do not use enormous blast furnaces or complex pollution-control equipment. Their production process uses the high-powered electric-arc furnace and the continuous caster. This process uses 9.9 million BTU's of energy to make one ton of steel, whereas the large integrated producers use 35.2 million BTU's.

The three plants and existing sales districts are located in Charlotte, North Carolina; Greenville, South Carolina; and Marietta, Georgia.

For the current year, Lucore estimated the following financial figures:

Sales District	Sales ($1,000)	Contribution ($1,000)
North Carolina	$ 6,000	$ 2,500
South Carolina	4,000	1,500
Georgia	5,000	2,000
	$15,000	$ 6,000

Fixed cost was $2,000,000.

Net profit was $4,000,000.

Lucore is considering opening a new sales district in Jackson, Mississippi. The comptroller estimates that the new district will obtain $2,500,000 in sales the first year and a contribution of $500,000. When the Mississippi district opens, the sales of the Georgia district are estimated to decline by 20%, with a 30% decline in contribution for the first year.

Compute sales, contribution, and net profit for the first year if Lucore opens up the new office in Mississippi.

© 1986 by Prentice-Hall, A Division of Simon & Schuster, Inc.
Englewood Cliffs, N.J. 07632. All rights reserved.
Printed in the United States of America.

Basic Concepts to Apply

Contribution = Sales - Variable Costs

Net Profit = Contribution - Fixed Costs

Break-Even Point = $\dfrac{\text{Fixed Costs}}{\text{Unit Sales Price - Unit Variable Costs}}$

Fixed Costs: The cost is fixed if it remains constant over a relevant range even when the volume of activity varies.

Variable Costs: The cost is variable if it changes when the volume of activity changes.

Sales _____

Contribution _____

Net Profit _____

Exercise 22-2

QUANTITATIVE ANALYSIS: DISTRIBUTION
CASE PROBELM--Rehm and Rooney
Industrial Distributors Company

Problem

The Rehm and Rooney Company was started in 1891, and manufactures and sells all types of bolts and screws for a great variety of industrial customers. The industry is in the mature stage of the product-life cycle, and there is considerable pressure for greater efficiency. The president of Rehm and Rooney is more concerned today with the net profit of the company than with a larger market share of a declining industry.

An intensive cost-accounting analysis of the major channels of distribution used by Rehm and Rooney for the last 40 years revealed the following figures:

Channel	Sales	Variable Costs	Contribution
A	$ 5,000,000	$ 3,500,000	$1,500,000
B	3,000,000	2,000,000	1,000,000
C	3,000,000	2,500,000	500,000
D	2,000,000	2,500,000	(500,000)
Total	$13,000,000	$10,000,000	$2,500,000

Fixed cost was $2,000,000.

Net profit was $500,000.

Basic Concepts to Apply

Contribution = Sales - Variable Costs

Net Profit = Contribution - Fixed Costs

$$\text{Break Even Point} = \frac{\text{Fixed Costs}}{\text{Unit Sales Price - Unit Variable Costs}}$$

Fixed Costs: The cost is fixed if it remains constant over a relevant range even when the volume of activity varies.

Variable Costs: The cost is variable if it changes when the volume of activity changes.

© 1986 by Prentice-Hall, A Division of Simon & Schuster, Inc.
Englewood Cliffs, N.J. 07632. All rights reserved.
Printed in the United States of America.

1. Compute sales, contribution, and net profit if channel D is eliminated.

    Sales _____

    Contribution _____

    Net Profit _____

2. Further cost-analysis indicated that channel C had a number of marginal customers with annual sales under $5,000. If Rehm and Rooney eliminated the marginal customers in channel C, the estimated sales would be $2,000,000, with estimated variable costs of $1,200,000.

    Compute sales, contribution, and net profit if channel D is eliminated and the marginal customers in channel C are eliminated.

    Sales _____

    Contribution _____

    Net Profit _____

Exercise 22-3

QUANTITATIVE ANALYSIS: DISTRIBUTION
CASE PROBLEM--Hartman Company (Wholesaler)

Problem

The Hartman Company is a full-line wholesaler selling both food and non-food products to retail grocery stores. In recent years, the Hartman Company has continued to add additional non-food products to its total product line. The company has 12 large retail stores in virtually all parts of the United States. The warehouses have been fully computerized for distribution efficiency. Hartman is considered a very successful wholesaler in terms of innovative management. Breaking down its contribution by major type of customer, the Hartman Company developed the following financial figures:

Type of Customer	Sales ($1,000)	Contribution ($1,000)
Supermarket Chains	$ 50,000	$ 6,000
Convenience Stores	20,000	3,000
Large Independents	50,000	9,000
Small Independents	40,000	2,000
	$160,000	$20,000
Less Fixed Costs		12,000
Net Profit		$ 8,000

Because the small independents are contributing very little because of small orders, the marketing manager is recommending raising the prices for small orders, requiring a minimum order size from the retailers, and limiting the number of sales calls to small retailers. The marketing manager anticipates that sales to small independents will drop $10,000,000, with a new contribution of $2,500,000.

Compute sales, contribution, and net profit if the marketing manager's recommendations are implemented.

© 1986 by Prentice-Hall, A Division of Simon & Schuster, Inc.
Englewood Cliffs, N.J. 07632. All rights reserved.
Printed in the United States of America.

Basic Concepts to Apply

Contribution = Sales - Variable Costs

Net Profit = Contribution - Fixed Costs

$$\text{Break Even Point} = \frac{\text{Fixed Costs}}{\text{Unit Sales Price} - \text{Unit Variable Costs}}$$

Fixed Costs: The cost is fixed if it remains constant over a relevant range even when the volume of activity varies.

Variable Costs: The cost is variable if it changes when the volume of activity changes.

Sales _____

Contribution _____

Net Profit _____

Exercise 22-4   QUANTITATIVE ANALYSIS: DISTRIBUTION
                                       CASE PROBLEM--Anson Industrials

        Anson Industrials is a manufacturer of eighteen different models of
industrial grinding, boring and gear-cutting machines and had sales of
$60 million last year. Prices for these machines vary from $9000 to $73,000.
The machines are sold through the Anson sales force and also through
selected manufacturers' agents. Thirty salespeople sold directly to
machine-tool users and provided 75% of the company's sales. On the average,
salespeople receive a base salary of $30,000 and have other expenses (trav-
eling, fringe benefits, supervision, office) amounting to $20,000. Sixty
manufacturing agents, each with exclusive territories, also represented
Anson Industrials. The agents were franchised in geographical areas where
the company did not do enough business to warrant the use of the direct
sales force. The manufacturing agent received a discount of 12.5% off list
price for all Anson machines that they sold.

        Compute the following:

1. What is the average annual sales figure per salesperson?

        _____

2. What is the average annual sales figure per manufacturing agent?

        _____

3. What is the cost of the Anson sales force (ignoring the manufacturers'
    agents) as a percentage of their sales?

        _____

4. What is the cost of the manufacturers' agents as a percentage of
    sales?

        _____

5. What is the breakeven point in sales per territory where it would pay
    Anson Industrials to replace a manufacturers' agent with a salesperson
    (considering costs exclusively)?

        _____

© 1986 by Prentice-Hall, A Division of Simon & Schuster, Inc.
Englewood Cliffs, N.J. 07632. All rights reserved.
Printed in the United States of America.   145

Exercise 23-1   CHANNEL CONFLICT

Two major types of channel conflict are 1) horizontal channel conflict and 2) vertical channel conflict. <u>Horizontal channel conflict</u> refers to conflict between firms at the same level of the channel. Two examples are 1) conflicts between two retailers and 2) conflicts between two producers. <u>Vertical channel conflict</u> refers to conflict between firms at different levels of the same channel. Two examples are 1) conflicts between the producer and retailer and 2) conflicts between the producer and the whole-saler.

Instructions: Read each of the following statements and indicate which type of conflict is primarily in-volved. Select only one for each statement.

	Horizontal Channel Conflict	Vertical Channel Conflict
1. A large manufacturer of plumbing products started to sell directly to large builders of homes and apartments. The plumbing wholesalers were extremely displeased be-cause they were being bypassed.	( )	( )
2. Procter & Gamble, a giant manufacturer of a wide line of grocery items, test-marketed Vibrant, a new laundry bleach. Clorox, which produces over 50 percent of the market for both liquid and pow-dered bleach is preparing for the mar-keting fight of its life.	( )	( )
3. A number of chain discount retailers stopped buying appliances from General Electric because the retailers were un-happy with the size of the discount General Electric was granting.	( )	( )
4. Macy's and Gimbel's department stores in New York City have a long history of com-petitive conflict. Both retail chains have claimed that they will not be under-sold.	( )	( )
5. Before it went bankrupt, Braniff Inter-national accused American Airlines of a series of "dirty tricks." The Civil Aeronautics Board investigated the	( )	( )

	Horizontal Channel Conflict	Vertical Channel Conflict

charges that American dumped several million dollars worth of Braniff debts on a ticket clearing house.

6. MediClinic is a freestanding emergency clinic that competes with general hospital emergency rooms and family doctors' offices. These new types of emergency clinics are heavily criticized by hospital administrators apparently without effect.   ( )   ( )

7. The national Holiday Inn Corporation has been criticized by a group of Holiday Inn franchisees, who have been restricted from building Holiday Inns outside their assigned territory.   ( )   ( )

8. General Motors threatened to pull the franchise agreement of a number of Chevrolet dealers in Southern California who were not complying with pricing, service, and promotion directives from GM.   ( )   ( )

9. Stratmar Systems offers manufacturers a combined cooperative refund promotion program. It publishes refund offers rather than coupons in best-food-day editions of 136 newspapers, replacing discount coupons that many retailers find too time-consuming to handle at checkout counters.   ( )   ( )

10. Seymour Merrin, owner of ComputerWorks, Inc., a chain of Connecticut computer stores called Apple Computer Inc.'s decision to drop its top-of-the-line business computer, the 3995 MacIntosh XL, "baffling." Just three months earlier, Apple renamed it and launched a major marketing campaign.   ( )   ( )

11. By eliminating butchers and meat counters, and by requiring customers to select packages from boxes on pallets and bag their own groceries, Richard Welton's Pick 'n Save warehouse food store increased its sales 40%. The head of his trade association considers it all a fad.   ( )   ( )

© 1986 by Prentice-Hall, A Division of Simon & Schuster, Inc. Englewood Cliffs, N.J. 07632. All rights reserved. Printed in the United States of America.

Exercise 23-2   CHANNEL CONFLICT

Two major types of channel conflict are 1) horizontal channel conflict and 2) vertical-channel conflict. <u>Horizontal channel conflict</u> refers to conflict between firms at the same level of the channel. Two examples are 1) conflicts between two retailers and 2) conflicts between two producers. <u>Vertical-channel conflict</u> refers to conflict between firms at different levels of the same channel. Two examples are 1) conflicts between the producer and retailer and 2) conflicts between the producer and the wholesaler.

Instructions: Read each of the following statements and indicate which type of conflict is primarily involved. Select only one for each statement.

	Horizontal Channel Conflict	Vertical Channel Conflict
1. GrandMa's Food, Inc., was recently acquired by Frito-Lay. GrandMa's Cookies is going after the mass-appeal market dominated by Nabisco cookies.	( )	( )
2. A Chevrolet dealer in Williamson, Michigan, was unhappy that General Motors was not shipping him enough Chevrolets. The Chevrolet zone manager said that GM was not punishing the dealer for selling cars for $50 over dealer's cost.	( )	( )
3. A number of Pontiac dealers in Houston, Texas, were very upset with a Pontiac dealer, Gray Pontiac. Gray consistently priced his Pontiac cars lower than the other dealers'.	( )	( )
4. Coors Beer put price-cutting retailers on notice that the retailers would be refused an adequate supply of beer if they did not follow the prices suggested by Coors.	( )	( )
5. W. and J. Sloane, a major furniture retailer, sold an expensive Hendron sofa for $1,483. Blackwelder, a discount retailer, sold the same Henredon sofa for $992.60. The manager of a Sloane store complained that Blackwelder did not maintain an expensive showroom or provide the decorator	( )	( )

	Horizontal Channel Conflict	Vertical Channel Conflict

expertise that Sloane provided for its customers.

6. The Target retailing chain sold Panasonic videotape recorders for $649, which was $200 less than the suggested retail price. A Panasonic sales executive felt that its quality image was diluted and that the action bordered on the irresponsible. ( )   ( )

7. Bekins Company is providing its household-moving customers with information packets about their new communities. Allied Van Lines charged that Bekins is offering a service without a charge in violation of federal trucking regulations. ( )   ( )

8. PepsiCo threatened its bottlers who also carry Seven-Up with violation of their executive franchise arrangements if botlers promoted the Seven-Up campaign attacking the safety of caffeine in soft drinks. ( )   ( )

9. Iowa Beef Producers Inc. grew from scratch into the world's largest slaughterer of beef cattle in less than 15 years. It sprinted ahead of old line packers such as Swift and Armour by shipping beef cut-up and packed in boxes instead of "swinging" in whole carcasses. It reduced shipping costs and eliminated the job of skilled meat-cutter at the store. ( )   ( )

10. Eighteen Coca-Cola bottlers sued Coca-Cola Co. in 1983 claiming that CC refused to deliver Diet Coke syrup unless they sign an amendment to their contracts requiring them to pay more for Diet Coke syrup than for standard syrup even though they claim Diet Coke syrup costs less to make. ( )   ( )

11. After announcing its intention in 1984 to replace its franchised dealers with factory-owned retail outlets, Porsche AG, maker of expensive sports cars, backed down from its plan. A group of dealers representing 80% of Porsche cars sold in the U.S. had sued Porsche over the proposed change. ( )   ( )

© 1986 by Prentice-Hall, A Division of Simon & Schuster, Inc.
Englewood Cliffs, N.J. 07632. All rights reserved.
Printed in the United States of America.

Exercise 23-3   CHANNEL CONFLICT

　　　Two major types of channel conflict are 1) horizontal channel conflict and 2) vertical channel conflict. Horizontal channel conflict refers to conflict between firms at the same level of the channel. Two examples are 1) conflicts between two retailers and 2) conflicts between two producers. Vertical channel conflict refers to conflict between firms at different levels of the same channel. Two examples are 1) conflicts between the producer and retailer and 2) conflicts between the producer and the whole- saler.

　　　　　　Instructions: Read each of the following statements and indicate which type of conflict is primarily in- volved. Select only one for each statement.

	Horizontal Channel Conflict	Vertical Channel Conflict
1. Some large supermarket chains have been un- happy with the trade policies of Procter & Gamble. One supermarket executive charges that P&G is rigid and arrogant in its policies.	( )	(✓)
2. Dentalworks operates retail dental centers in New Jersey and Pennsylvania. These re- tail centers are condemned as undesirable and unethical by certain independent den- tists in both states.	(✓)	( )
3. After Gillette introduced its new Erasemate pen in 1979, Sripto introduced the Scripto erasable pen in 1980. Both companies sued each other for patent in- fringement. The suits were eventually settled out of court.	(✓)	( )
4. Most franchise agreements require the franchise holder to purchase needed sup- plies from the franchisor. Some fran- chise holders have gone to court in an effort to obtain freedom to select suppliers.	( )	( )
5. Many independent gasoline retailers sell- ing Arco gasoline feel that they have been unfairly treated by the Atlantic Richfield Company, which produces Arco products.	( )	( )

	Horizontal Channel Conflict	Vertical Channel Conflict

They were unhappy when Arco credit cards were discontinued.

6. A number of major supermarket chains in Chicago engaged in a 14-month price war in the 1970s. Jewel Food, Dominicks, and National Tea all had lower earnings or larger losses because of the price cuts at the retail level.	( )	( )
7. Sony, one of the world's largest manufacturers of television sets, is strongly opposed to transshipments of its sets. Transshipping occurs when one retailer buys a large order to qualify for quantity discounts and then sells part of the shipment to another retailer.	( )	( )
8. Sizzling over an advertising campaign in 1982 that compared McDonald's Big Macs unfavorably with Burger King's Whoppers, McDonald's filed suit in federal court to keep Burger King's commercial off the air.	( )	( )
9. When Levi Strauss & Co. changed its distribution strategy and began selling to Sears, J. C. Penney and other mass merchandisers, R. H. Macy & Co., a major department-store chain, stopped carrying Levi apparel.	( )	( )
10. When Tenneco, Inc., which operated JI Case Farm Implements, bought International Harvester Corp. in 1984, it reduced the number of Case and IH dealerships by 15% because of territorial overlaps. Kirby's O.K. Implement, which had been a Case retailer, sued Tenneco for loss of its franchise area.	( )	( )
11. Trying to regain lost share of market, Weingarten, a grocery chain, launched an advertising campaign comparing its new, lower prices to Kroger's. In its ads, Weingarten identified Kroger as the market leader with the lowest prices and said Weingarten would match Kroger. The campaign was unsuccessful and Weingarten sold its stores.	( )	( )

© 1986 by Prentice-Hall, A Division of Simon & Schuster, Inc.
Englewood Cliffs, N.J. 07632. All rights reserved.
Printed in the United States of America.

Exercise 24-1   VERTICAL-MARKETING SYSTEMS

Three types of vertical marketing systems are 1) corporate, 2) admin-
istered, and 3) contractual. A <u>corporate vertical-marketing system</u> com-
bines the successive stages of production and distribution under one
ownership for complete control and coordination. An <u>administered vertical
marketing system</u> is coordinated not through ownership but through the
relative power of one member of the system who dominates the relationship
and achieves control because of company size or strength of brand name.
A <u>contractual vertical-marketing system</u> achieves coordination and control
through formal agreements or contracts. Three main types of contractual
systems are 1) retail-sponsored cooperatives, 2) wholesaler-sponsored
cooperatives, and 3) franchise organizations.

Instructions: Read each of the following statements
and indicate which VMS is described.

	Corporate	Administered	Contractual
1. Associated Grocers, a cooperative, has been formed by a group of re- tailers to coordinate their purchases and to perform wholesaling functions for their members.	( )	( )	( )
2. Because of its size and expertise, the Frigidaire Appliance Division of General Motors is able to obtain excellent cooperation from re- tailers.	( )	( )	( )
3. H&R Block is a national concern specializing in assisting individ- uals or families in the prepara- tion of their income tax returns. Local offices are operated by independent business people who are bound by formalized agreements.	( )	( )	( )
4. Thomas & Shiff is a large food wholesaler. To maintain its growth, the firm has purchased two retail chains that operate a total of 39 outlets in its geographic area.	( )	( )	( )
5. Kraft Foods has developed a space management program for retailers that suggests an optimal alloca- tion of space in supermarket dairy	( )	( )	( )

cases. Most supermarkets follow
the suggested allocation, aware
that Kraft's products provide
approximately 60 percent of the
sales from the typical case, exclusive of eggs, butter, and milk.

6. Florsheim Shoes, a quality brand of   (   )   (   )   (   )
   men's shoes, are manufactured by the
   Florsheim Company which operates
   its own vast organization of retail
   shoe shops across the United States

7. McDonald's charges an initial fee   (   )   (   )   (   )
   of about $150,000 for rights to a
   franchise. In exchange, the local
   operator receives detailed manuals
   and joint buying economies on meat,
   buns, and supplies.

8. The Firestone Tire and Rubber Com-   (   )   (   )   (   )
   pany owns and operates 1,250 of its
   retail stores.

9. Procter & Gamble manufactures High   (   )   (   )   (   )
   Point decaffeinated coffee, Puritan
   cooking oil, Sure deodorant, and
   Crest toothpaste. P&G enjoys excellent cooperation from its retailers because of the consumer
   acceptance of these brands.

10. Stating, "We want to bring to the   (   )   (   )   (   )
    club business what Holiday Inn
    brought to the hotel business,"
    McFaddin Ventures Inc. opened its
    eighteenth unit of Confetti's, a
    club for singles. Disk jockeys
    must adhere to a headquarters list
    of records and decor has been pain-
    stakingly programmed to attract fe-
    males. Knowing that singles are
    fickle customers, McFaddin plans to
    close all units within a year and
    reopen with a new theme at that time.

11. In May of 1985, Nabisco Brands Inc.   (   )   (   )   (   )
    requested that trading in its stock
    be halted. The firm was holding
    merger talks with R. J. Reynolds.
    Reynolds was interested in shelf
    space power in the supermarket
    and Nabisco would give it a larger
    presence in the food business.

© 1986 by Prentice-Hall, A Division of Simon & Schuster, Inc.
Englewood Cliffs, N.J. 07632. All rights reserved.
Printed in the United States of America.

Exercise 24-2   VERTICAL-MARKETING SYSTEMS

   Three types of vertical marketing systems are 1) corporate, 2) admin-
istered, and 3) contractual. A <u>corporate vertical marketing system</u> com-
bines the successive stages of production and distribution under one
ownership for complete control and coordination. An <u>administered vertical
marketing system</u> is coordinated not through ownership but through the
relative power of one member of the system who dominates the relationship
and achieves control because of company size or strength of brand name.
A <u>contractual vertical-marketing system</u> achieves coordination and control
through formal agreements or contracts. Three main types of contractual
systems are 1) retail-sponsored cooperatives, 2) wholesaler-sponsored
cooperatives, and 3) franchise organizations.

          Instructions: Read each of the following statements
          and indicate which VMS is described.

	Corporate	Administered	Contractual
1. Procter & Gamble manufactures Sure deodorant, Charmin bathroom tissue, Pampers diapers, Coast deodorant soap, and High Point decaffeinated coffee. Because of the consumer acceptance of these brands, retailers are eager to carry them.	( )	( )	( )
2. Hart, Shafner & Marx, a manufacturer of quality men's clothing, owns and operates over 250 retail stores carrying its line exclusively.	( )	( )	( )
3. Avis Rent-A-Car grants local business people the right to operate under the Avis name as well as to receive requests for car rentals from other cities through the Avis organization, in exchange for an initial fee and a percentage of the volume.	( )	( )	( )
4. The Gulf Oil Corporation owns and operates a large proportion of its gasoline service stations.	( )	( )	( )
5. IGA (Independent Grocers Alliance) was developed by a large wholesale grocery firm to offer independent grocers joint buying economies in exchange for their agreeing to	( )	( )	( )

	Corporate	Administered	Contractual
consolidate their purchases through IGA.			

6. Although Heinz and Lipton have challenged the Campbell Soup Company in the marketing of soup, the Campbell firm enjoys strong consumer acceptance that results in retailers' giving premium shelf space to Campbell's products and cooperating fully in its promotion.

	( )	( )	( )

7. Kentucky Fried Chicken grants rights to own and operate individual outlets in exchange for an initial payment and a share of the income from the licensed sites. Over 500 outlets have been opened outside the United States under this procedure, in addition to the many operating within this country.

	( )	( )	( )

8. In 1978, the Tandy Corporation started manufacturing its TRS-80 personal computer, which it now distributes through the more than 6,500 Radio Shack retail stores. Radio Shack is a division of the Tandy Corporation.

	( )	( )	( )

9. Montgomery Ward, because of its vast number of retail stores, its purchasing power, and its acceptance by retail customers, is able to obtain attractive prices and terms from suppliers.

	( )	( )	( )

10. Faced with rising costs and increased competition, many small, local firms are engaging in "conversion franchising." It was pioneered by Century 21, a California real-estate company to enlist local real-estate firms under its umbrella.

	( )	( )	( )

11. Super Valu is the nation's largest food wholesaler. Over 1,970 retail food stores voluntarily enter into a purchasing agreement with Super Valu. They also receive a variety of operational and administrative services enabling them to compete with chains.

	( )	( )	( )

© 1986 by Prentice-Hall, A Division of Simon & Schuster, Inc. Englewood Cliffs, N.J. 07632. All rights reserved. Printed in the United States of America.

155

NAME *Joseph Lopez*

Exercise 24-3   VERTICAL MARKETING SYSTEMS

Three types of vertical marketing systems are 1) corporate, 2) admin-
istered, and 3) contractual. A <u>corporate vertical-marketing system</u> com-
bines the successive stages of production and distribution under one
ownership for complete control and coordination. An <u>administered vertical
marketing system</u> is coordinated, not through ownership, but through the
relative power of one member of the system who dominates the relationship
and achieves control because of company size or strength of brand name.
A <u>contractual vertical marketing system</u> achieves coordination and control
through formal agreements or contracts. Three main types of contractual
systems are 1) retail-sponsored cooperatives, 2) wholesaler-sponsored
cooperatives, and 3) franchise organizations.

Instructions: Read each of the following statements
and indicate which VMS is described.

	Corporate	Administered	Contractual
1. In exchange for the right to oper-ate a local Burger King, the local franchise holder must agree not only to pay the initial franchise fee, but also must operate the local outlet in accordance with the terms of the contract.	( )	( )	(✓)
2. Magnavox, a manufacturer of quality televisions and radios, has ob-tained excellent cooperation and support from its independent re-tailers because of the retailers' desire to maintain the Magnavox brand in their line.	( )	(✓)	( )
3. The Exxon Company owns and operates a large proportion of its Exxon Car Care Centers and self-service sta-tions.	(✓)	( )	( )
4. When the Norge Division of the Borg-Warner Corporation suggests that its independent retailers fol-low Norge's recommended inventory control plan, most do. Norge be-lieves that retailers cooperate because of the value of its line.	( )	( )	( )
5. The largest food wholesaler in the U.S. is Super Valu Stores, Inc. It has more than 1,500 independent	( )	( )	(✓)

food retailers who have entered
into voluntary buying agreements
with Super Valu.

6. Holiday Inns has tried to develop   ( )   ( )   ( )
    an integrated operation that in-
    cludes its own carpet mills and a
    furniture manufacturing plant to
    supply its motels and inns.

7. Brooks Brothers, a subsidiary of   ( )   ( )   ( )
    Allied Stores Corporation, manu-
    factures a large portion of the
    (predominantly men's) clothing it
    sells through the 35 stores it owns
    and operates.

8. The Oldsmobile Division of General   ( )   ( )   (✓)
    Motors Corporation signs formal
    agreements with its dealers grant-
    ing them the right to sell its
    cars.

9. Because of its large number of re-   ( )   ( )   ( )
    tail stores, its mass purchasing
    power, and its consumer acceptance,
    Sears, Roebuck & Company finds it-
    self the dominant member of the
    channel.

10. Coca-Cola Co. owns only about 10%   ( )   ( )   ( )
    of its U.S. bottling operations.
    The remainder are 300 independents
    whose contracts give them their
    franchises in perpetuity. Recently,
    Coke managed to oversee changes in
    about 120 territories by offering
    or withdrawing marketing funds and
    by persuasion, including helping to
    arrange financing for buyouts by
    aggressive replacements.

11. Ben & Jerry's Homemade, Inc., a   ( )   ( )   ( )
    Burlington, Vermont, firm that
    sold just $4 million in ice cream
    in 1983, sued Pillsbury, whose
    Haagen-Daas subsidiary dominates
    the superpremium ice cream market.
    B&J claim that HD told some dis-
    tributors to drop other super-
    premium brands or lose HD which
    outsells B&J 10-to-1 where both
    are sold.

© 1986 by Prentice-Hall, A Division of Simon & Schuster, Inc.
Englewood Cliffs, N.J. 07632. All rights reserved.
Printed in the United States of America.

Exercise 25-1   DISTRIBUTION COVERAGE

Three types of distribution coverage for goods and services are 1) intensive, 2) selective, and 3) exclusive. <u>Intensive distribution</u> is an effort by producers to obtain widespread exposure in as many outlets as possible, although this generally means that the producer will have to give up much of its channel control. The product will also have minimal dealer support. <u>Selective distribution</u> is an effort by producers to reduce the number of dealers but increase the volume of sales per dealer. This strategy aims at maintaining some channel control and an attractive brand image with a reduced number of distributors. The distributors selected provide promotional support, either through store reputation, quality of salespeople, attractive location or depth of stock. <u>Exclusive distribution</u> is the most restrictive form of distribution by producers. Generally only one dealer will be appointed in a given geographic territory. The producer obtains, in exchange, maximum dealer sales effort.

Instructions: Analyze each of the following statements and indicate which type of distribution is primarily involved. Select only one.

	<u>Intensive</u>	<u>Selective</u>	<u>Exclusive</u>
1. Sizes of camera film that will fit popular types of cameras are displayed in racks near the cashier's counter in grocery stores, drug stores, and convenience stores. Racks are maintained by rack jobbers rather than by the retailers.	( )	( )	( )
2. In Southeast Texas, the new Mondeal 8 Ferrari automobile, a two-plus-two sports coupe, is available only at Ferrari of Houston at 6541 Southwest Freeway.	( )	( )	( )
3. Baccarat crystal requires special handling and sales effort because of its construction and cost. Very expensive because of its uniqueness, only a few stores in a market area carry the product.	( )	( )	( )
4. Imported Iranian caviar is so expensive and appeals to such a small group that stores will handle it only if granted complete rights to distribute it in a given market area.	( )	( )	( )
5. Miller Lite Beer is distributed in	( )	( )	( )

taverns, restaurants, grocery stores, liquor stores, and convenience stores under a policy of mass advertising and competitive prices.

6. The perfume Les Must de Cartier comes in a removable smoked-glass bottle encased in an 18-karat gold frame. Replacement bottles are sold only through a small number of department stores in each market because the originator of the perfume wishes to maintain some control over its distribution.

( )   ( )   ( )

7. Wrigley's Spearmint gum is available in special self-service displays in a wide variety of retail outlets.

( )   ( )   ( )

8. The designer Geoffrey Been distributes his floor-length, midnight blue, quilted silk chiffon and velour striped coats only through one outlet per market. The coat retails for about $2,500.

( )   ( )   ( )

9. Albert Van Liat manufactures a high quality wallpaper. Only a small amount of each design is produced. Known as "the ultimate fashion statement," these unique colors and designs are distributed only through interior design studios.

( )   ( )   ( )

10. Learning that greeting card manufacturer Hallmark has signed an agreement with J. C. Penney to be Penney's exclusive supplier of cards, American Greeting of Cleveland signed a similar agreement with Sears.

( )   ( )   ( )

11. During the energy shortages in the 1970's, Winnebago Industries produced a motor home, the "Itasca," priced lower than its Winnebago model. It was sold through an entirely new dealer organization. The roughly 300 Winnebago dealers found their exclusive dealerships were not as exclusive as they thought they were.

( )   ( )   ( )

© 1986 by Prentice-Hall, A Division of Simon & Schuster, Inc. Englewood Cliffs, N.J. 07632. All rights reserved. Printed in the United States of America.

Exercise 25-2   DISTRIBUTION COVERAGE

Three types of distribution coverage for goods and services are 1) intensive, 2) selective, and 3) exclusive. <u>Intensive distribution</u> is an effort by producers to obtain widespread exposure in as many outlets as possible, although this generally means that the producer will have to give up much of its channel control. The product will also have minimal dealer support. <u>Selective distribution</u> is an effort by producers to reduce the number of dealers but increase the volume of sales per dealer. This strategy aims at maintaining some channel control and an attractive brand image with a reduced number of distributors. The distributors selected provide promotional support, either through store reputation, quality of salespeople, attractive location, or depth of stock. <u>Exclusive distribution</u> is the most restrictive form of distribution by producers. Generally only one dealer will be appointed in a given geographic territory. The producer obtains, in exchange, maximum dealer sales effort.

Instructions: Analyze each of the following statements and indicate which type of distribution is primarily involved. Select only one.

	<u>Intensive</u>	<u>Selective</u>	<u>Exclusive</u>
1. Sub-Zero brand refrigerators and freezers for kitchen built-ins will blend with any interior by accepting front and side panels to match your decor. This brand is available only at custom kitchen remodeling centers located in major shopping centers.	( )	( )	( )
2. Waterford goblets are handblown and hand-cut. The Waterford Crystal company has a historical heritage. Waterford is sold only through a small number of stores, because of the need for salespeople trained in its quality and care.	( )	( )	( )
3. The Jenn-Air cooking system is a high-priced convection cooking device that permits users to char-grill steaks and other foods indoors. It is sold through a limited number of retail stores.	( )	( )	( )
4. The very expensive Leica 35mm camera is only sold by one retailer in any market. The camera has four automatic modes and one manual override that requires considerable photographic experience.	( )	( )	( )

	Intensive	Selective	Exclusive

5. Small Everyday batteries, packaged two or four together, are available for retail purchase in special racks near the cashier's counter in grocery outlets, drug stores, and convenience stores. ( ) ( ) ( )

6. People Magazine, an upscale gossip publication with informal photographs of celebrities, is sold in racks stocked by rack jobbers in grocery stores, drug stores, and convenience stores. ( ) ( ) ( )

7. With a V-12 engine, the 262 horsepower Jaguar XJ-S automobile lists for $34,000 in the United States. Only one dealer is appointed for each major market because of the investment in tools, service facilities, and parts required relative to the number sold. ( ) ( ) ( )

8. Gillette Supermax Pro 1500-watt hair dryer is available at self-service counters in drug stores, variety stores, catalog stores, department stores, discount stores, and some grocery stores. ( ) ( ) ( )

9. Expensive chinaware is handled through a limited number of retailers throughout the country. Only one retailer handles the chinaware in a particular geographical area. ( ) ( ) ( )

10. Automobile manufacturers sell most of their cars through franchised dealers. Manufacturers also sell directly to rental firms, some of whom buy over 150,000 cars each year. Hertz regularly resells part of its used fleet through more than 100 retail outlets, some of which are located near new-car dealers. ( ) ( ) ( )

11. Retail Dental Centers has nine dental franchises in the Minneapolis-St. Paul area, all in enclosed shopping malls. Prices are 10-to-50% lower and the beeper Johnny's mother picked up at the dentist will call her when her son is finished. ( ) ( ) ( )

© 1986 by Prentice-Hall, A Division of Simon & Schuster, Inc. Englewood Cliffs, N.J. 07632. All rights reserved. Printed in the United States of America.

Exercise 25-3

DISTRIBUTION COVERAGE

Three types of distribution coverage for goods and services are 1) intensive, 2) selective, and 3) exclusive. <u>Intensive distribution</u> is an effort by producers to obtain widespread exposure in as many outlets as possible, although this generally means that the producer will have to give up much of its channel control. The product will also have minimal dealer support. <u>Selective distribution</u> is an effort by producers to reduce the number of dealers but increase the volume of sales per dealer. This strategy aims at maintaining some channel control and an attractive brand image with a reduced number of distributors. The distributors selected provide promotional support, either through store reputation, quality of salespeople, attractive location or depth of stock. <u>Exclusive distribution</u> is the most restrictive form of distribution by producers. Generally only one dealer will be appointed in a given geographic territory. The producer obtains, in exchange, maximum dealer sales effort.

Instructions: Analyze each of the following statements and indicate which type of distribution is primarily involved. Select only one.

	Intensive	Selective	Exclusive
1. In 1982, the Aramis brand of men's toiletries, a high margin item for retailers, was available primarily through department stores.	( )	( )	( )
2. Camel cigarettes are sold not only at most convenience stores, drug stores, and grocery stores, but also in vending machines, restaurants, bars, and plants.	( )	( )	( )
3. The magazine <u>TV Guide</u> is usually found in racks at the cashier's counter in grocery outlets, drug stores, and convenience stores. Should it be sold out, the retailer does not restock.	(✓)	( )	( )
4. Hood brand sails for sailboats are internationally known for their fine quality and careful design. Hood sails are sold through only one retail outlet in each major area.	( )	( )	(✓)
5. Known by automobile experts as one of the world's finest automobiles, the Rolls Royce can be purchased only from one dealer in a major	( )	( )	( )

city. There is no representation in
smaller communities, and only one
dealer in major cities because of the
investment in tools, parts, and service facilities required relative
to the number sold.

6. The high price of private airplanes,   ( )   (✓)   ( )
    the need for no-compromise servicing,
    and a narrow market results in only
    a few dealers in most cities being
    authorized by the Cessna Aircraft
    Company.

7. Gulf is substantially reducing the   ( )   ( )   ( )
    number of neighborhood gasoline
    service stations. The result is
    cleaner, more attractive stations
    with tighter supervisory control.

8. Coca-Cola has widespread distribu-   ( )   ( )   ( )
    tion, including vending machines
    that may, in high-demand areas, be
    placed next to Pepsi Cola machines.

9. Designer clothes by Jack Mulqueen, of   ( )   ( )   ( )
    100% pure silk crepe de chine are
    available only at one store in each
    market.

10. Mary Cammarata, a grey-haired grand-   ( )   ( )   ←(✓)
    mother, grossed more than $100,000
    selling women's underwear. Using
    live models, she displays items
    at bars and clubs that cater to
    businessmen at lunch and feature
    scantily clad dancers.

11. One of America's best known cloth-   ( )   ( )   ( )
    ing manufacturer markets two lines
    of suits that are identical except
    for the labels. The retailers,
    often geographically competitive,
    are granted "exclusive" retailing
    rights to one of the lines.

© 1986 by Prentice-Hall, A Division of Simon & Schuster, Inc.
Englewood Cliffs, N.J. 07632. All rights reserved.
Printed in the United States of America.

163

Exercise 26-1   TYPES OF WHOLESALERS

Wholesaling functions are performed by middlemen who resell products to retailers or to industrial, institutional, or governmental institutions for their use. Three major groups of middlemen performing wholesaling functions are 1) merchant wholesalers, 2) agents and brokers, and 3) manufacturers' and retailers' branches. <u>Merchant wholesalers</u> are independently owned businesses that take title to the product they sell. Two types of merchant wholesalers are full-service wholesalers and limited-service wholesalers. <u>Brokers and agents</u> are independently owned businesses that do not take title to the products they sell and rarely handle them. Three types of agents and brokers are manufacturers' agents, selling agents, and resident buyers. <u>Manufacturers' and retailers' branches</u> are not independently owned businesses. Manufacturers' sales branches conduct wholesaling and distribution functions and are owned by the manufacturer. Retailer buying branches conduct buying functions and are owned by the retailer.

Instructions: Analyze each of the following statements and indicate which type of wholesaler is described. Select only one for each statement.

	Merchant Wholesalers	Brokers and Agents	Manufacturers' and Retailers' Branches
1. Stewart and Stevenson manufactures diesel engines for industrial purposes. The company owns Stewart and Stevenson Services, Engine Division, which has warehouses in all major cities to carry inventory, provide credit terms, and maintain an aggressive sales force.	( )	( )	( )
2. Leggett and Sons sells industrial chemicals to the paint industry. Leggett's eight salesmen call on many small paint manufacturers. Leggett does not take title, nor does it maintain inventory.	( )	( )	( )
3. The Sherwin-Williams Company manufactures a wide line of household paints, automotive finishes, and industrial coatings. It sells its paints through a national network of Sherwin-Williams retail stores.	( )	( )	( )
4. Bob Herbert & Associates serves as the Southwest representative for seven manufacturers of oil-well	( )	( )	( )

	Merchant Whole-salers	Brokers and Agents	Manufacturers' and Retailers' Branches

equipment. Herbert handles ball valves, mud guns, and pressure hoses. Herbert sells on consignment and arranges for delivery direct from the manufacturers.

	Merchant Whole-salers	Brokers and Agents	Manufacturers' and Retailers' Branches
5. Lawson Product sells over 17,000 different types of fasteners (screws, bolts, crimps, etc.) through 1,000 Lawson salespersons. The firm has five regional warehouses. It purchases from a variety of manufacturers and takes title to its stock.	( )	( )	( )
6. The Vallen Corp. specializes in plant safety equipment, taking title to over 6,000 items ranging from acid hoods to vapor sniffers. It sells to industrial plants on the Gulf Coast.	( )	( )	( )
7. The Office Products Division of IBM offers typewriters, word processors, and computers through its district sales offices to a wide variety of business users.	( )	( )	( )
8. Gibson Electronics Supply is a large Los Angeles-based distributor of semiconductors, resistors, and capacitors. It owns its inventory and has eighteen branches.	( )	( )	( )
9. Coldwell Banker, a nationwide real-estate company, operates both commercial and residential divisions. The firm charges the seller a commission but does not take title.	( )	( )	( )
10. Automotive Search, Inc., in Rockville, Maryland, charges $190 for finding a car that the buyer wants and for negotiating a price. Records indicate customers pay an average of $100 over dealer's invoice.	( )	( )	( )

© 1986 by Prentice-Hall, A Division of Simon & Schuster, Inc. Englewood Cliffs, N.J. 07632. All rights reserved. Printed in the United States of America.

Exercise 26-2   TYPES OF WHOLESALERS

Wholesaling functions are performed by middlemen who resell products to retailers or to industrial, institutional, or governmental institutions for their use. Three major groups of middlemen performing wholesaling functions are 1) merchant wholesalers, 2) agents and brokers, and 3) manufacturers' and retailers' branches. Merchant wholesalers are independently owned businesses that take title to the product they sell. Two types of merchant wholesalers are full-service wholesalers and limited-service wholesalers. Brokers and agents are independently owned businesses that do not take title to the products they sell and rarely handle them. Three types of agents and brokers are manufacturers' agents, selling agents, and resident buyers. Manufacturers' and retailers' branches are not independently owned businesses. Manufacturers' sales branches conduct wholesaling and distribution functions and are owned by the manufacturer. Retailer buying branches conduct buying functions and are owned by the retailer.

Instructions: Analyze each of the following statements and indicate which type of wholesaler is described. Select only one for each statement.

	Merchant Whole-salers	Brokers and Agents	Manufacturers' and Retailers' Branches
1. I. E. Shapero is responsible for selling the entire output of several noncompeting textile mills located in South Carolina. The Shapero Company completes all of the wholesale functions for these firms on an exclusive basis, but does not take title or possession of the output of the mills.	( )	( )	( )
2. Stokes Supplies offers a limited line of basic office supplies to Atlanta's office supply retailers. Stokes does not offer delivery or credit and has no outside sales force. Stokes does take title to items in its inventory.	( )	( )	( )
3. American Service Company is an independent company carrying nearly all of the products needed by a hardware retailer. ASC provides trade credit, takes title to its inventory, and provides a delivery service to retailers.	( )	( )	( )

	Merchant Whole-salers	Brokers and Agents	Manufacturers' and Retailers' Branches
4. Lone Star Supply Company furnishes a wide variety of repair parts and pipes to oil-well drilling contractors, oil companies, and shipyards. It is a subsidiary of Lone Star Steel Company, which produces oil-field pipe.	( )	( )	( )
5. C & J, Inc., maintains an inventory of nearly 10,000 items used by hospitals, nursing homes, and clinics. It guarantees a zero-out-of-stock policy on certain health care items. Credit is extended for 60 days, and C & J has title for its vast inventory.	( )	( )	( )
6. Sanchez-Hammersmith represents several manufacturers in New York City and carries noncompetitive, complementary lines of gear-cutting machines, grinding machines, and boring machines. The firm has 12 salespeople, all of whom are compensated on a commission basis. SH does not take title or offer credit.	( )	( )	( )
7. The IBM Corporation sells a wide line of computer hardware and programming software direct to industrial firms by means of IBM's district sales office.	( )	( )	( )
8. Johnson's Travel Agency arranges for airline and cruise tickets. They offer credit and free delivery of tickets to your home or office, but do not buy the tickets from the airlines.	( )	( )	( )
9. American Airlines has a staff of marketing representatives that contact business organizations to encourage the use of American Airlines for business travel. They also arrange for corporate discounts and priority handling.	( )	( )	( )

© 1986 by Prentice-Hall, A Division of Simon & Schuster, Inc. Englewood Cliffs, N.J. 07632. All rights reserved. Printed in the United States of America.

Exercise 26-3   TYPES OF WHOLESALERS

Wholesaling functions are performed by middlemen who resell products to retailers or to industrial, institutional, or governmental institutions for their use. Three major groups of middlemen performing wholesaling functions are 1) merchant wholesalers, 2) agents and brokers, and 3) manufacturers' and retailers' branches. <u>Merchant wholesalers</u> are independently owned businesses that take title to the product they sell. Two types of merchant wholesalers are full-service wholesalers and limited-service wholesalers. <u>Brokers and agents</u> are independently owned businesses that do not take title to the products they sell and rarely handle them. Three types of agents and brokers are manufacturers' agents, selling agents, and resident buyers. <u>Manufacturers' and retailers' branches</u> are not independently owned businesses. Manufacturers' sales branches conduct wholesaling and distribution functions, and are owned by the manufacturer. Retailer buying branches conduct buying functions and are owned by the retailer.

Instructions: Analyze each of the following statements and indicate which type of wholesaler is described. Select only one for each statement.

	Merchant Whole-salers	Brokers and Agents	Manufacturers' and Retailers' Branches
1. Foremost Foods, Inc., specializes in distributing health foods. It provides trade credit, maintains an extensive assortment, which it owns, and has its own sales force that sells to health-food retailers in New England.	( )	( )	( )
2. The DeMontrand Sales Division sells all products manufactured by the parent company, the DeMontrand Wire and Cable Company. It is completely responsible for field selling.	( )	( )	( )
3. Sunset West sells nonprescription drugs and cosmetics to variety stores and small supermarket chains in the Southeast. Sunset's salespeople set up displays, refill shelves with pricemarked merchandise Sunset has title to, and calculate the amount due from each individual store at the time of delivery.	( )	( )	( )
4. Mahaand Sons has the territorial rights in southern California to	( )	( )	( )

	Merchant Whole-salers	Brokers and Agents	Manufacturers' and Retailers' Branches

the distribution of a number of food items. Its eight-person sales force calls on chain-store buyers. The Mahaand company does not take title and does not provide credit, but does store and deliver the line it represents.

5. Parke-Ashford gets building materials from manufacturers and arranges for shipment directly to Parke-Ashford's clients in Chicago. P-A does not take physical possession or title.	( )	( )	( )
6. Charles Schwab & Co. is the largest discount stock brokerage firm in the United States. A member of the New York Stock Exchange, it offers securities, stocks, and bonds through offices coast-to-coast.	( )	( )	( )
7. The W-K-M Division of ACF Industries sells complete oilfield wellheads, gate valves, butterfly valves, and plug valves it manufactures through regional sales offices that also arrange for repairs and services.	( )	( )	( )
8. Bartley Builders Hardware, Inc., has a complete line of locks, cabinet hardware, sinks, and faucets that it has purchased from manufacturers, and offers them for resale to builders and hardware retailers.	( )	( )	( )
9. Federated Department Stores, a large chain of department stores, maintains buying offices in New York City so that it can rapidly complete consolidated purchases of garments for resale through the chain.	( )	( )	( )
10. National Content Liquidators, Inc., liquidates industrial plants, hospitals, and hotels. Generally the firm contracts to conduct a liquidation sale, not an auction. NCL's share is a percentage of the proceeds but the firm does provide the seller with a guaranteed lump sum.	( )	( )	( )

© 1986 by Prentice-Hall, A Division of Simon & Schuster, Inc.
Englewood Cliffs, N.J. 07632. All rights reserved.
Printed in the United States of America.

Exercise 27-1

QUANTITATIVE ANALYSIS: PROMOTION
CASE PROBLEM--Collogena Corporation

Problem

Collogena Corporation manufactures and sells Collogena, a brand of "medicinal" soap. Collogena's headquarters near Los Angeles International Airport has simple production facilities. Return on equity has averaged 21% over the last five years. Collogena is found principally in drugstores.

For the current year, the Collogena comptroller estimated the following financial figures:

Collogena case sales	1,800,000
Price per case to drug wholesalers	$15.00
Recommended price per case to drugstores	18.50
Recommended price per case to consumers	28.00

Costs

Plant Overhead	$1,000,000
Administration overhead	3,000,000
Marketing overhead	2,000,000
Production cost per case	$6.00
Sales and distribution costs per case	$3.00
Advertising Appropriation	$2,000,000

Basic Concepts to Apply

$$\text{Contribution} = \text{Sales} - \text{Variable Costs}$$

$$\text{Net Profit} = \text{Contribution} - \text{Fixed Costs}$$

$$\text{Break-Even Point} = \frac{\text{Fixed Costs}}{\text{Unit Sales Price} - \text{Unit Variable Costs}}$$

Fixed Costs: The cost is fixed if it remains constant over a relevant range even when the volume of activity varies.

Variable Costs: The cost is variable if it changes when the volume of activity changes.

1. Compute sales, contribution, and net profit for the current year.

    Sales _____

    Contribution _____

    Net Profit _____

2. What is the break-even point in case sales for the current year if we do no advertising?

    Break-even point _____

3. What is the break-even point in case sales for the current year if we follow our intention of spending $2,000,000 on advertising?

    Break-even point _____

© 1986 by Prentice-Hall, A Division of Simon & Schuster, Inc.
Englewood Cliffs, N.J. 07632. All rights reserved.
Printed in the United States of America.

Exercise 27-2   QUANTITATIVE ANALYSIS: PROMOTION
                                       CASE PROBLEM--RMX Corporation

The RMX Corporation is a manufacturer of printing equipment. The company has five salespeople who call on large printing firms throughout the United States. The industry has been growing at the rate of 15% over the last five years. The comptroller developed the following financial figures for the current year.

Salesperson	Sales	Contribution
A	$6,000,000	$1,400,000
B	4,500,000	700,000
C	5,000,000	800,000
D	4,500,000	600,000
E	5,000,000	1,000,000

Fixed cost was $2,000,000.

1. Compute sales, contribution, and net profit.

                    Sales _____

             Contribution _____

               Net Profit _____

2. Management is considering opening up a new sales territory. For the first year, sales are estimated at $1,200,000 with a contribution of $50,000. In addition, the fixed cost would increase $150,000. Compute sales, contribution, and net profit if the new territory is added.

                    Sales _____

             Contribution _____

               Net Profit _____

NAME _____

Exercise 27-3

QUANTITATIVE ANALYSIS: PROMOTION
CASE PROBLEM--Tom Brown Legal Clinics

Tom Brown Legal Clinics have pioneered the use of advertising in the legal profession. Brown's commercials are simple and conservative. Thirty-second television spots invite people to bring their wills and divorces to Tom Brown Legal Clinics.

For the current year, the following financial conditions existed:

Number of wills handled	50,000
Number of divorces handled	150,000
Price charged per will	$ 50.00
Price charged per divorce	100.00
Legal and processing cost per will	$ 20.00
Legal and processing cost per divorce	60.00
Office rental	$2,000,000
General Administration	1,000,000
Advertising	1,500,000

1. Compute sales, contribution, and net profit for the current year.

Sales _____

Contribution _____

Net Profit _____

© 1986 by Prentice-Hall, A Division of Simon & Schuster, Inc.
Englewood Cliffs, N.J. 07632. All rights reserved.
Printed in the United States of America.

2. The advertising agency is recommending that Tom Brown spend an additional $200,000 to promote the need for wills. Management estimated that an additional 20,000 wills could be generated by the additional advertisements. Compute sales and net profit if the advertising expenditure is made.

Sales _____

Net Profit _____

Exercise 27-4

QUANTITATIVE ANALYSIS: PROMOTION
CASE PROBLEMS-- ArcWeld Company

The ArcWeld Company is an industrial distributor of a wide line of electrical and plumbing products. The company sells in a mature industry, with future industry growth around 2 percent annually. The president is dissatisfied with the sales performance of the sales force.

For the current year, the following financial conditions existed:

Salespeople	Sales	Contribution
1	$2,000,000	$450,000
2	1,000,000	50,000
3	1,200,000	350,000
4	2,200,000	420,000
5	1,800,000	350,000
6	1,800,000	380,000

Fixed cost was $1,500,000.

1. Compute sales, contribution, and net profit.

Sales _____

Contribution _____

Net Profit _____

© 1986 by Prentice-Hall, A Division of Simon & Schuster, Inc.
Englewood Cliffs, N.J. 07632. All rights reserved.
Printed in the United States of America.

2. The president was very unhappy with the performance of salesman #2. In addition, the sales territory for salesman #2 was considered marginal because of the lack of any large city in the sales territory.

Compute sales, contribution, and net profit if salesman #2 is fired and his sales territory is eliminated.

Sales _____

Contribution _____

Net Profit _____

Exercise 27-5

QUANTITATIVE ANALYSIS: PROMOTION
CASE PROBLEM--Moore Manufacturing
Corp.

Problem

Moore Manufacturing Corporation produces a variety of packaging machines to a wide group of industrial companies. With 250 salespersons located throughout the United States and Canada, the national sales manager has developed a number of key measures and indexes to measure the performance of the sales force. Key measures include:

$$\text{Sales Performance Index} = \frac{\text{Actual Sales}}{\text{Sales Quota}} \times 100$$

$$\text{Order/Call Ratio} = \frac{\text{Total Orders}}{\text{Total Calls}} \times 100$$

$$\text{Average Sales per Order} = \frac{\text{Actual Sales}}{\text{Total Orders}}$$

$$\text{Sales Commission} = 12\% \text{ of Actual Sales}$$

At the end of the current year, the following selling information was obtained:

Salesperson	Sales Quota	Actual Sales	Total Calls	Total Orders
A	$ 800,000	$ 400,000	1,000	300
B	600,000	250,000	400	200
C	500,000	500,000	1,100	600
D	800,000	900,000	1,300	1,000
E	300,000	450,000	500	400
TOTAL	$3,000,000	$2,500,000	4,300	2,500

© 1986 by Prentice-Hall, A Division of Simon & Schuster, Inc.
Englewood Cliffs, N.J. 07632. All rights reserved.
Printed in the United States of America.

1. Complete the following table:

Salesperson	Sales Performance Index	Order/Call Ratio	Average Sales Per Order	Sales Commissions
A	_____	_____	_____	_____
B	_____	_____	_____	_____
C	_____	_____	_____	_____
D	_____	_____	_____	_____
E	_____	_____	_____	_____
Average for all Salespeople	_____	_____	_____	_____

2. On the basis of your analysis, who are the two best salespersons?

_____

3. On the basis of your analysis, who are the two worst salespersons?

_____

Exercise 28-1   MARKETING—COMMUNICATIONS MIX

The marketing communication mix consists of 1) advertising, 2) personal selling, 3) publicity, and 4) sales promotion. <u>Advertising</u> is any <u>paid</u> form of nonpersonal presentation of ideas, goods, or services by an identified sponsor. <u>Personal selling</u> is an oral presentation in a conversation with one or more prospective purchasers for the purpose of making sales. <u>Publicity</u> is nonpersonal stimulation of demand by communicating news about the organization or its products or services in a medium without having to pay for the news. <u>Sales promotion</u> involves activities, other than advertising, personal selling, or publicity, that stimulate interest and purchase. It includes such activities as point-of-purchase displays, contests, trading stamps, trade shows, and distribution of samples.

Instructions: Analyze each of the following statements and indicate which communication tool applies. Select only one tool.

	Adver- tising	Personal Selling	Pub- licity	Sales Promotion
1. When anyone orders flowers for a birthday from Lee's Flower Shoppe, clerks also suggest a dozen helium-filled balloons.	( )	( )	( )	( )
2. Radio Shack provides props to TV studios at no charge for use in such programs as "Hill Street Blues," "Greatest American Hero," and others. Management estimated that its products achieved five billion exposures in 1982.	( )	( )	( )	( )
3. Republic Airlines offers children between two and sixteen years of age airline tickets in exchange for five proofs-of-purchase sales from Ralston Purina cereals.	( )	( )	( )	( )
4. When more than 1000 students attended the 1985 International Conference of the collegiate chapters of the American Marketing Association, the AMA published photos and a story in that organization's national newspaper <u>Marketing News</u>.	( )	( )	( )	( )
5. For a $20 donation to the National Multiple Sclerosis Society, the donor will receive a free calendar	( )	( )	( )	( )

© 1986 by Prentice-Hall, A Division of Simon & Schuster, Inc.
Englewood Cliffs, N.J. 07632. All rights reserved.
Printed in the United States of America.

179

	Adver- tising	Personal Selling	Pub- licity	Sales Promotion
that contain 326 baseball player card reproductions.	( )	( )	( )	( )
6. Many outstanding high school athletes select their colleges as a result of a personal visit by the college's coach to the athlete's home.	( )	( )	( )	( )
7. In 1982, Brown & Williamson Tobacco Co. developed a new national marketing campaign tying its Kool brand of cigarettes to contemporary music and featuring magazine ads depicting jazz musicians with the slogan, "There's only one way to play it . . . Kool."	( )	( )	( )	( )
8. Coca Cola adopted a new theme, "Coke is it!" in 1982, featuring an emphasis on taste. Each TV commercial had seven scenes establishing anticipation-reward-refreshing taste sequences.	( )	( )	( )	( )
9. In its effort to dislodge the lead of Lever Bros.' Wisk in liquid heavy-duty detergents, Procter & Gamble distributed $1 coupons in 225 newspapers across the country. P&G has traditionally relied on coupons to promote trial of new products.	( )	( )	( )	( )
10. After placing gigantic pictures of athletes in mid-motion in large posters and wall paintings, the sporting shoe and apparel firm Nike observed considerable newspaper coverage of its campaign. One Los Angeles paper even printed a map showing where the boards were located.	( )	( )	( )	( )
11. Ticket Holder Marketing supplies free ticket jackets to airlines plus approximately $300,000 per year. In turn, THM sells space on the jackets to such concerns as Dollar Rent A Car Systems.	( )	( )	( )	( )

Exercise 28-2   MARKETING COMMUNICATIONS MIX

The marketing communication mix consists of 1) advertising, 2) personal selling, 3) publicity, and 4) sales promotion. <u>Advertising</u> is any <u>paid</u> form of nonpersonal presentation of ideas, goods, or services by an identified sponsor. <u>Personal selling</u> is an oral presentation in a conversation with one or more prospective purchasers for the purpose of making sales. <u>Publicity</u> is nonpersonal stimulation of demand by communicating news about the organization or its products or services in a medium without having to pay for the news. <u>Sales promotion</u> involves activities other than advertising, personal selling, or publicity that stimulate interest and purchase. It includes such activities as point-of-purchase displays, contests, trading stamps, trade shows, and distribution of samples.

Harvey's, the largest department store in the state, is a part of Consolidated Stores, a national chain of department stores. The store yearly devotes approximately 4.3 percent of sales to its communications mix. The merchandising division has planned a special storewide, month-long event featuring a Chinese theme.

Instructions: Analyze each of the following statements and indicate which communication tool applies. Select only one tool.

	Adver-tising	Personal Selling	Pub-licity	Sales Promotion
1. The store plans a full-page insert displaying Chinese products each of the city's daily newspapers.	( )	( )	( )	( )
2. The <u>Daily Chronicle</u>, the major newspaper, printed a news article on the background of the Chinese promotion at Harvey's, featuring several hundred years of Chinese history.	( )	( )	( )	( )
3. The personnel division arranged for the temporary transfer of several sales employees of Chinese ancestry to the China department and trained them so they could explain to customers the intricacies of the Chinese imports.	( )	( )	( )	( )
4. Patrons of the store's two restaurants received free Chinese fortune cookies. Some of the cookies contained certificates for valuable free merchandise.	( )	( )	( )	( )

© 1986 by Prentice-Hall, A Division of Simon & Schuster, Inc.
Englewood Cliffs, N.J. 07632. All rights reserved.
Printed in the United States of America.

	Advertising	Personal Selling	Publicity	Sales Promotion
5. Three times each day, the store presented a demonstration of Chinese cooking in the kitchenware department.	( )	( )	( )	( )
6. On the evening prior to the event, the store held a ball at the Chinese consulate, which was reported extensively on the society page of the newspapers.	( )	( )	( )	( )
7. Representatives from China flew to the U.S. to explain to prospective customers the craftsmanship of Chinese rugs which were available for purchase.	( )	( )	( )	( )
8. Special mailings describing the higher-priced jade jewelry items were sent to charge account customers who lived in the more affluent sections of town.	( )	( )	( )	( )
9. All charge account customers received a notice along with their monthly bill statements from Harvey's describing a $250 discount on a round trip airline ticket to Peking, China, for everyone who purchased $500 or more in Chinese merchandise during the month-long event.	( )	( )	( )	( )
10. On the first day of the event, the mayor was invited to cut a ribbon at the front door of the store. Two of the three major local TV stations carried the event on their evening news programs.	( )	( )	( )	( )
11. All charge account customers received a notice along with their monthly bill statements from Harvey's describing a special collection of Chinese evening gowns available for purchase.	( )	( )	( )	( )
12. In response to a request from a famous rock star who was appearing in concert, several store employees brought some of the more unusual items of clothing to the star's hotel suite for her examination. She purchased several.	( )	( )	( )	( )

Exercise 28-3   MARKETING COMMUNICATIONS MIX

The marketing communication mix consists of 1) advertising, 2) personal selling, 3) publicity, and 4) sales promotion. <u>Advertising</u> is any <u>paid</u> form of nonpersonal presentation of ideas, goods, or services by an identified sponsor. <u>Personal selling</u> is an oral presentation in a conversation with one or more prospective purchasers for the purpose of making sales. <u>Publicity</u> is nonpersonal stimulation of demand by communicating news about the organization or its products or services in a medium without having to pay for the news. <u>Sales promotion</u> involves activities,other than advertising, personal selling, or publicity,that stimulate interest and purchase. It includes such activities as point-of-purchase displays, contests, trading stamps, trade shows, and distribution of samples.

Competition among the hospitals in New Orleans, Louisiana, for registered nurses is severe. In an effort to attract nurses to the Meadowcrest Hospital, the administrative board has considered the following actions.

Instructions: Analyze each of the following statements and indicate which communication tool applies. Select only one tool.

	Adver-tising	Personal Selling	Pub-licity	Sales Promotion
1. Conducting a contest among the nurses currently employed by the hospital and awarding prizes to those who supplied the best list of prospective nurse employees.	( )	( )	( )	( )
2. Running a series of ads in the New Orleans <u>Times-Picayune</u> newspaper under the theme "Nursing Made Easy" to attract readers to the field of nursing.	( )	( )	( )	( )
3. The hospital's associate administrator speaks to a regular meeting of the New Orleans Nursing Association on new developments at the hospital, in the hope that some of those attending will wish to join Meadowcrest.	( )	( )	( )	( )
4. The personnel director visits regional nursing schools to interview and recruit prospective graduates.	( )	( )	( )	( )
5. The hospital's executive responsible	( )	( )	( )	( )

© 1986 by Prentice-Hall, A Division of Simon & Schuster, Inc.
Englewood Cliffs, N.J. 07632. All rights reserved.
Printed in the United States of America.   183

	Adver- tising	Personal Selling	Pub- licity	Sales Promotion

for marketing arranges for a local
television station to do a feature
story on the superior emergency
room facilities.

6. The administrative board considers ( ) ( ) ( ) ( )
   offering a free get-away weekend
   at the Royal Orleans Hotel to all
   nursing personnel at other hospitals
   who join Meadowcrest Hospital during
   its current recruitment drive.

7. A direct mail campaign stressing ( ) ( ) ( ) ( )
   nursing as a career is aimed at
   parents of high school seniors who
   are enrolled in certain nearby
   schools.

8. When a very popular rock and roll en- ( ) ( ) ( ) ( )
   tainer on a tour had to enter Meadow-
   crest Hospital for an emergency ap-
   pendectomy, the local newspaper pub-
   lished an interview with the concert
   star, featuring a picture of him
   with several Meadowcrest nurses.

9. The hospital's marketing executive ( ) ( ) ( ) ( )
   was approached by a producer of
   video tapes who proposed producing
   a 12-minute tape of the hospital
   that could be loaned to prospective
   patients to reduce their possible
   fears about entering the hospital
   and to show the quality of nursing
   care.

10. Every time the hospital runs an ad, ( ) ( ) ( ) ( )
    a copy of it is sent to 600 ran-
    domly selected registered nurses in
    the New Orleans area.

11. The marketing director is considering ( ) ( ) ( ) ( )
    sponsoring a softball team consisting
    of male and female nurses from the
    hospital to demonstrate the quality of
    life of employees at Meadowcrest.

12. A member of the marketing staff has ( ) ( ) ( ) ( )
    prepared a story about several nurses
    who had retired from nursing but have
    come back to work at Meadowcrest be-
    cause a shorter work week was available. He
    hopes the Times-Picayune newspaper will use it.

Exercise 29-1   PROMOTION APPROPRIATION
                                       DETERMINATION

    Four common methods of determining the total size of the promotion budget are 1) affordable funds, 2) percentage of sales, 3) competitive-parity, and 4) objective-and-task. The <u>affordable-funds</u> method is basically the managers determining what they feel the company can afford to spend. The amount is apt to vary widely from year to year and is often arbitrary. In the <u>percentage of sales</u> approach, promotional dollars are determined either by applying a certain percentage figure to current or anticipated dollar sales or a set dollar amount is established to be applied to anticipated unit sales, such as an amount for each automobile sold. The <u>competitive-parity</u> method requires the organization to match the proportion of gross sales a competitor spends or to match the industry average. The fourth approach, <u>objective-and-task</u>, is increasing in use because it attempts to tie the dollar expenditures to specific communications tasks that need to be performed. The appropriation is the sum of the estimated costs of performing these tasks.

        Instructions: Analyze each of the following statements and indicate which appropriation or budget method is described.

		AF	%S	CP	O&T
1.	The advertising manager of Nathan's, a leading women's specialty store, determines her next year's advertising expenditure by applying to the store's forecasted sales a proportion that reflects the industry's typical figure. The figure is available annually from the National Retail Merchant's Association.	( )	( )	( )	( )
2.	When the Four Seasons opened its new luxury 400-room hotel in downtown Houston in 1981, the advertising manager arrived at his budget by planning to expose each of the season ticket holders from such groups as the symphony and the opera to three advertising impressions. He also planned to invite the chief executive officers of several corporations to be his guests at luncheons where they would become acquainted with the hotel and its services.	( )	( )	( )	( )
3.	After purchasing the Joseph Schlitz Brewery, the new management prepared an optimistic sales forecast for Schlitz Light beer. When sales did not reach expected levels, the	( )	( )	( )	( )

© 1986 by Prentice-Hall, A Division of Simon & Schuster, Inc.
Englewood Cliffs, N.J. 07632. All rights reserved.
Printed in the United States of America.

planned advertising had to be reduced
accordingly.

4. To improve on 1982's disappointing sales   ( )   ( )   ( )   ( )
    figures, Detroit automakers introduced and
    advertised sporty, high-performance models
    in 1983. Budgets were based on expected
    costs of making targeted segments aware of
    the features of the new cars, and not on
    historical patterns.

5. The Reverend Billy Lawson has scheduled   ( )   ( )   ( )   ( )
    religious sermons on Wednesday nights for
    college students. He promotes them by
    placing an ad in the campus weekly news-
    paper. The size of the ad is dependent
    upon the contributions received at the
    previous Wednesday session.

6. Trudy Stone, manager of the junior dress   ( )   ( )   ( )   ( )
    department of Gold's department store,
    plans her advertising over a six-month
    period. She multiplies her forecasted
    sales figure by a proportion of the sales
    to obtain her advertising budget.

7. Hand Percivale owns a gun shop. Although   ( )   ( )   ( )   ( )
    he would like to match in dollars the pro-
    motional spending of Bobbie Clark's Guns,
    which is the biggest gun shop in town, he
    has been unable to do so. Hank ends up
    advertising heavily when media grant him
    special discounts and drops advertising
    when he has to pay normal rates.

8. Top management of the Deter Corporation   ( )   ( )   ( )   ( )
    listed eight objectives they wish to achieve
    in this year's advertising. After review by
    the advertising manager, they reduce the num-
    ber to three, and approved the funds they
    thought necessary to achieve them.

9. Because of an oversight, the owners of La   ( )   ( )   ( )   ( )
    Crema, a new, small ice cream shop,
    neglected to budget funds for advertising.
    After consultation, they applied to promo-
    tion cash from their depreciation reserves.

Exercise 29-2

PROMOTION APPROPRIATION
DETERMINATION

Four common methods of determining the total size of the promotion budget are 1) affordable funds, 2) percentage of sales, 3) competitive-parity, and 4) objective-and-task. The <u>affordable funds</u> method is basically the managers determining what they feel the company can afford to spend. The amount is apt to vary widely from year to year and is often arbitrary. In the <u>percentage of sales</u> approach, promotional dollars are determined either by applying a certain percentage figure to current or anticipated dollar sales or a set dollar amount is established to be applied to anticipated unit sales such as an amount for each automobile sold. The <u>competitive-parity</u> method requires the organization to match the proportion of gross sales a competitor spends or to match the industry average. The fourth approach, <u>objective-and-task</u>, is increasing in use because it attempts to tie the dollar expenditures to specific communications tasks that need to be performed. The appropriation is the sum of the estimated costs of performing these tasks.

       Instructions: Analyze each of the following statements and indicate which appropriation or budget method is described.

	AF	%S	CP	O&T
1. Capital Airlines increased its advertising by 50 percent in 1985 to promote its low-cost transatlantic fares. Management, observing that the U.S. dollar was stronger, expected an increase in Americans going abroad. Capital estimated a fifty-percent increase in sales and appropriated a corresponding amount for advertising.	( )	( )	( )	( )
2. Disney World in Florida opened its new Epcot Center in the fall of 1982. Management planned its promotion to insure that, within 30 days, a certain percentage of prospective visitors would be aware of the opening date and could state two attractive aspects of the center when polled.				
3. Although Mars, Inc., a competitor of Hershey's, spends approximately 9% of its sales on advertising, Hershey Foods feels that the quality of its items and its excellent support by retailers permits it to maintain its industry leader position in sales although Hershey spends only one-third of Mars' amount.	( )	( )	( )	( )

© 1986 by Prentice-Hall, A Division of Simon & Schuster, Inc.
Englewood Cliffs, N.J. 07632. All rights reserved.
Printed in the United States of America.

	AF	%S	CP	O&T

4. Being severely limited on funds, the three partners in a new restaurant decided to rely on word-of-mouth communication to promote the quality of their authentic French cuisine. They plan to devote funds to advertising when they are better able to do so. ( ) ( ) ( ) ( )

5. Although 1982 was an unprofitable year for most airlines, the competition under deregulation was so severe that none of the firms reduced their advertising budgets, preferring to spend the industry average. ( ) ( ) ( ) ( )

6. In 1980 the cigarette producers Philip Morris, Inc., R. J. Reynolds Industries, and the American Tobacco Company all devoted roughly the same percentage of sales income to advertising. ( ) ( ) ( ) ( )

7. The Anheuser-Busch brewery arrived at an advertising appropriation for the introduction of the Budweiser Light brand by first estimating the number of beer drinkers the firm wanted to have try the brand and then estimating the number of advertising exposures that would be necessary before a prospect would become aware of the new brand. ( ) ( ) ( ) ( )

8. Not having any industry guidelines, a state university had difficulty in determining an amount for advertising that the state legislature would find acceptable. An alumnus donated $1,000 in private funds for general use and this amount was allocated to promotion. ( ) ( ) ( ) ( )

9. After purchasing the Café Louie French restaurant from its original owners, the new management established an advertising budget. They first set the objective of achieving awareness of the restaurant by 30% of the residents of the city's affluent areas within 30 days, and a first-time visit within two months by 5% of those aware. ( ) ( ) ( ) ( )

Exercise 29-3   PROMOTION APPROPRIATION
                                 DETERMINATION

Four common methods of determining the total size of the promotion
budget are 1) affordable funds, 2) percentage of sales, 3) competitive-
parity, and 4) objective-and-task. The <u>affordable funds</u> method is basically
the managers determining what they feel the company can afford to spend.
The amount is apt to vary widely from year to year and is often arbitrary.
In the <u>percentage of sales</u> approach, promotional dollars are determined
either by applying a certain percentage figure to current or anticipated
dollar sales or a set dollar amount is established to be applied to anticipated unit sales such as an amount for each automobile sold. The
<u>competitive-parity</u> method requires the organization to match the proportion
of gross sales a competitor spends or to match the industry average. The
fourth approach, <u>objective-and-task</u>, is increasing in use because it attempts to tie the dollar expenditures to specific communications tasks that
need to be performed. The appropriation is the sum of the estimated costs
of performing these tasks.

Instructions: Analyze each of the following statements and indicate which appropriation or budget
method is described.

	AF	%S	CP	O&T

1. Pizza Hut, a subsidiary of Pepsico, has   ( ) ( ) ( ) ( )
    a national advertising program prepared
    by the Foote, Cone & Belding advertising
    agency, in addition to regional advertis-
    ing campaigns. Pizza Hut's national ad-
    vertising budget is determined by a two
    percent assessment on each unit's sales,
    and each franchise holder must spend an
    additional two percent for regional
    advertising.

2. A percentage-of-sales approach would pro-   ( ) ( ) ( ) ( )
    vide tire company B. F. Goodrich with an
    inadequate budget, because it is much
    smaller than industry giants Goodyear and
    Firestone. Goodrich concentrates its
    money to reach small but influential seg-
    ments. It promotes its high-tech T/A tire
    by inserting ads in car magazines and by
    sponsoring car races where drivers of high
    performance and recreational cars gather.

3. Tom Hazard and his dad opened a retail   ( ) ( ) ( ) ( )
    motorcycle store, also dealing in parts
    and service. His dad enjoys seeing the
    name of the firm on outdoor posters and

© 1986 by Prentice-Hall, A Division of Simon & Schuster, Inc.
Englewood Cliffs, N.J. 07632. All rights reserved.
Printed in the United States of America.   189

he rented 20 poster boards for several
months until he exhausted their cash
reserve.

4. Hazel Blake is a vice president for adver-   ( ) ( ) ( ) ( )
   tising and promotion of a small department
   store in San Jose, California. She planned
   her six-month promotion budget by checking the median operating figures for stores
   of a similar size. The information was
   provided by the National Retail Merchants'
   Association.

5. Mr. Oscar Bigg inherited control of the Big   ( ) ( ) ( ) ( )
   Blast Brewery when his father died. Oscar
   enjoys planning the firm's advertising and
   supervising its TV commercials. He sets
   his budget by averaging the amount spent
   by competitors on a per-barrel basis and
   multiplying this by his expected output.

6. By the end of 1982, twenty-seven outlets   ( ) ( ) ( ) ( )
   had been opened nationally by People's
   Restaurant. Preferring to devote scarce
   financial resources to site location and
   improved operating systems, they spent
   limited amounts on advertising depending
   on available cash.

7. The Reliance Bank & Trust Company desired   ( ) ( ) ( ) ( )
   that within six months 50% of the local re-
   tail merchants be able to identify it as
   the bank that has the largest dollar revenues in the community. The bank budgeted
   sufficient funds to expose each merchant to
   four ads containing this message and
   achieved its goal.

8. The Northwest Utility Company provides   ( ) ( ) ( ) ( )
   electricity to a three-state area. It
   determines its advertising appropriation
   by applying to its expected revenues a
   percentage figure that in previous years
   has appeared to be adequate.

9. The Norman Boot Company has determined   ( ) ( ) ( ) ( )
   that it takes five exposures to an ad to
   obtain a purchase from a prospect. Five
   exposures cost ten cents per person per
   exposure. The firm plans to sell 1,000,000
   pairs of boots. The total appropriation
   needed is $50,000.

Exercise 30-1   PUSH/PULL STRATEGIES

Two basic promotional strategies for producers of consumer products
are 1) a push strategy and 2) a pull strategy. A <u>push strategy</u> calls for
the producer to develop a promotion mix that will push the product through
the channel system. The producer aims its promotion at the wholesalers
and retailers. Thus the product is pushed through the channel system.
A <u>pull strategy</u> calls for the producer to develop a promotion mix that will
pull the product through the channel system. The producer aims its promotion directly at the consumer, who will ask the retailer for the product.
Thus, the product is pulled through the channel system.

> Instructions: Analyze each of the following
> statements and indicate which strategy is
> primarily involved.

	<u>Push Strategy</u>	<u>Pull Strategy</u>
1. Perrier is a French company that sells mineral water to consumers. Perrier's U.S. subsidiary introduced its product in the United States in 1977. Almost all of the promotion effort went to TV commercials narrated by Orson Welles and to high-fashion women's magazines.	( )	( )
2. Toro Corporation is the largest manufacturer of snow throwers, which are used by consumers to remove snow from sidewalks and driveways. Most of its promotional dollars go to supporting its wholesalers and retailers in selling the snow throwers.	( )	( )
3. Frito-Lay spends the majority of its promotion mix on advertising aimed directly at consumers. A full array of television, magazine, and outdoor advertisements are combined into a massive promotional effort.	( )	( )
4. In selling its heating oil to home consumers, Texaco allocates the largest part of its promotion budget to its sales activities. The salesmen work closely with the independent oil jobbers, who sell and deliver the heating oil to the consumer.	( )	( )

© 1986 by Prentice-Hall, A Division of Simon & Schuster, Inc.
Englewood Cliffs, N.J. 07632. All rights reserved.
Printed in the United States of America.   191

	Push Strategy	Pull Strategy

5. Vassarette, which sells to the intimate apparel market, has traditionally allocated the bulk of its promotional budget to its sales force. The sales department works very closely with a wide range of retailers.   ( )   ( )

6. Polaroid Camera was heavily promoted to consumers in 1983 with a heavy emphasis on television advertisements. James Garner and Mariette Hartley continued to be the principal spokespeople in the ad.   ( )   ( )

7. Frank Perdue made Perdue Chickens a household name in the 1970s. Using aggressive and heavy consumer advertising in radio, newspapers, and magazines, the Perdue company increased chicken sales to consumers. Their slogan was, "It takes a tough man to make a tender chicken."   ( )   ( )

8. Alliance Manufacturing Company in Ohio produces a line of TV antenna equipment. Rather than aim a lot of promotional dollars at the consumer, Alliance spends money on salesmen to work closely with such large retail TV installers as RCA distributors.   ( )   ( )

9. According to Pharmaceutical Manufacturers Association, pharmaceutical companies, on the average, devote 70% of their promotional effort to the hiring of detail salespeople who call on doctors to provide literature and samples of drug products. The remaining 30% is devoted to journal advertising and to direct mail.   ( )   ( )

10. To win customers away from Eastern Airlines and People Express Airlines, New York Air offered free round-trip flights to any of its cities to passengers who completed three New York-Boston round-trips. The offer was made in a $1.5 million newspaper, radio and TV campaign.   ( )   ( )

Exercise 30-2   PUSH/PULL STRATEGIES

Two basic promotional strategies for producers of consumer products are 1) a push strategy and 2) a pull strategy. A <u>push strategy</u> calls for the producer to develop a promotion mix that will push the product through the channel system. The producer aims its promotion at the wholesalers and retailers. Thus the product is pushed through the channel system. A <u>pull strategy</u> calls for the producer to develop a promotion mix that will pull the product through the channel system. The producer aims its promotion directly at the consumer, who will ask the retailer for the product. Thus, the product is pulled through the channel system.

Instructions: Analyze each of the following statements and indicate which strategy is primarily involved.

		Push Strategy	Pull Strategy
1.	When Mead-Johnson first developed Metrecal, the firm positioned the product as a health product for people wanting to lose weight. Major promotional effort was aimed at doctors and pharmacists.	( )	( )
2.	Anacin is a popular brand of aspirin made by American Home Products. Television advertising aimed at consumers is the major promotional tool used in selling Anacin.	( )	( )
3.	Folger's Coffee has a weak share of market in the New York area, the nation's biggest single consumer market for coffee. Folger's mailed "rich" coupons for 45 cent discounts a can to four million households in the New York area.	( )	( )
4.	Binney and Smith sells Crayola products to people of all ages. With the largest part of their promotional budget in consumer advertising in 1982, Binney and Smith moved out of print and into Saturday morning TV shows and late afternoon programming, such as "Happy Days" reruns.	( )	( )
5.	Rheem sells residential gas water heaters through an elaborate	( )	( )

© 1986 by Prentice-Hall, A Division of Simon & Schuster, Inc. Englewood Cliffs, N.J. 07632. All rights reserved. Printed in the United States of America.

distribution network of plumbing
companies. The sales department pre-
pares elaborate promotional activities such as high-quality brochures
which are aimed at the distributor
and account for the largest part of
the promotion budget.

6. Texas Instruments used Bill Cosby in   ( )   ( )
   1982 as a spokesman for calculator
   products sold by TI. National television, the major media for the promotion of TI products, was aimed at
   the general consumer. The theme of
   the calculator campaign was, "What-
   ever you need to do with numbers,
   TI can help you better."

7. Texize Chemical Company sells such   ( )   ( )
   household cleaning products as
   Fantastik, Janitor-in-a-Drum,
   Simonize, and K2r. Texize uses
   trade premiums and promotional
   packages aimed at the retailer as
   its major promotional efforts in
   competing against Proctor & Gamble,
   Lever Brothers, and Colgate.

8. Schwinn Bicycle Company in Chicago   ( )   ( )
   has a ten percent share of the domes-
   tic bicycle market. Schwinn allo-
   cates the major part of its promotion
   budget to the sales force, which
   focuses on maintaining a quality
   group of distributors and retail
   dealers.

9. When Jordache Enterprises, Inc. at-   ( )   ( )
   tempted to enter the women's fashion
   jean business, they had difficulty
   convincing department stores to stock
   an additional brand. JEI advertised
   "The Jordache Look" in women's magazines, featuring a shirtless male
   model. Female shoppers took the ad
   to the stores looking for the brand.

10. When the Hanes Corporation introduced   ( )   ( )
    L'eggs pantyhose, it spent an adver-
    tising amount equal to that for a new
    cigarette or detergent introduction.
    Opening advertising was at a level twice
    as high as total advertising for the
    entire industry.

Exercise 30-3   PUSH/PULL STRATEGIES

Two basic promotional strategies for producers of consumer products
are 1) a push strategy and 2) a pull strategy. A <u>push strategy</u> calls for
the producer to develop a promotion mix that will push the product through
the channel system. The producer aims its promotion at the wholesalers
and retailers. Thus the product is pushed through the channel system.
A <u>pull strategy</u> calls for the producer to develop a promotion mix that will
pull the product through the channel system. The producer aims its promotion directly at the consumer, who will ask the retailer for the product.
Thus, the product is pulled through the channel system.

> Instructions: Analyze each of the following
> statements and indicate which strategy is
> primarily involved.

	Push Strategy	Pull Strategy
1. Fisher-Price toy company is a sub-sidiary of Quaker Oats company. New preschool toys introduced by Fisher-Price are heavily promoted in women's magazines and television, to both parents and children.	( )	( )
2. S. C. Johnson introduced Agree, a cream rinse and hair conditioner, to the personal-care market in 1977. They allocated most promotion effort to television advertising, magazine advertisement, and large sampling programs that put small bottles of Agree into the hands of 31 million women.	( )	( )
3. Prentice-Hall sells college textbooks to students in universities. The major promotional expenditures are for the sales force who call on the professors teaching in the universi-ties, for free textbooks given to professors, and for advertising aimed at the professors.	( )	( )
4. Neutrogena Corporation, in Los Angeles, sells "medicinal" soap, which is positioned somewhere be-tween fancy skin-care products and mundane toiletries. Rather than spend money on mass advertising	( )	( )

© 1986 by Prentice-Hall, A Division of Simon & Schuster, Inc.
Englewood Cliffs, N.J. 07632. All rights reserved.
Printed in the United States of America.

like Procter & Gamble does,
Neutrogena salesmen call on 5,000
dermatologists and leave samples of
the soap product.

5. Merck and Company of Rahway, New   ( )   ( )
    Jersey, sells a wide variety of drug
    products for consumers. Since most
    of these drugs must be prescribed by
    a doctor, Merck spends most of its
    promotional budget on detail sales-
    men. These detail salesmen call on
    doctors and provide samples of the
    drug products.

6. General Foods produces Kool-Aid, a   ( )   ( )
    powdered soft drink. The majority
    of the promotional mix goes to na-
    tional television advertising, which
    is directed at the children's mar-
    ket. Over twenty million dollars
    was spent in consumer advertising
    for Kool-Aid in 1979.

7. Carrier Air Conditioning has a high   ( )   ( )
    share of the market for home air con-
    ditioning in the United States.
    Carrier gives enormous promotional
    support to its distributors and re-
    tail dealers.

8. Dannon Yogurt is produced by Beatrice   ( )   ( )
    Foods. The major part of promotion
    for Dannon Yogurt is in national and
    local television. The major theme of
    the advertisement is the value of
    Dannon for weight control and for
    healthy bodies.

9. Executives of the Polaroid Corporation,   ( )   ( )
    producers of photographic and related
    products, felt television advertising
    was a major factor in the rapid ac-
    ceptance of the Polaroid camera in the
    United States market.

10. Because commercial television was not   ( )   ( )
    available in France in 1966 when the
    Polaroid Corporation planned to intro-
    duce the Polaroid Swinger model camera
    there, the company hired in-store
    demonstrators to visit retail stores
    on prearranged schedules to conduct
    demonstrations.

Exercise 31-1   THE SELLING PROCESS

Three major steps in the selling process are 1) pre-presentation, 2) presentation, and 3) follow-up. <u>Pre-presentation</u> includes the three steps of prospecting, qualifying, and preapproach learning. Prospecting is the process of identifying potential prospects. Qualifying is the process of screening prospects to see if they are worth pursuing further. Preapproach learning is the process of learning about the prospect company and its customers. <u>Presentation</u> includes the approach, the actual sales presentation, any demonstration, handling objections, and efforts to close. <u>Follow-up</u> includes checking to see that the product is delivered on time and installed properly, as well as determining if the buyer is satisfied and is using the purchased item properly.

        Instructions: Analyze each of the following statements and indicate which major step is involved. Select only one for each statement.

	Pre-presentation	Presentation	Follow-Up
1. A car salesperson used about fifty people to "bird-dog" for automobile shoppers leads. The salesperson paid $50 for every lead that resulted in a sale.	( )	( )	( )
2. A successful home-builder's salespeople call on new homeowners a month after they move into the new house. Any minor problems are immediately fixed.	( )	( )	( )
3. Warner and Swasey sells technical machinery to manufacturers. One of the major jobs of salesmen is to ensure that new machinery has been installed properly.	( )	( )	( )
4. Emery Air Freight gathers extensive market information about prospective customers before calling on these prospects.	( )	( )	( )
5. Salespeople for Cutco Company actively demonstrate the cutting ability of their knives by cutting different food products on a board in the prospect's home.	( )	( )	( )

© 1986 by Prentice-Hall, A Division of Simon & Schuster, Inc.
Englewood Cliffs, N.J. 07632. All rights reserved.
Printed in the United States of America.

	Pre-presentation	Presentation	Follow-Up
6. C. R. Daniels sells industrial textiles and materials-handling equipment. They use a film to illustrate the strengths and versatility of their products.	( )	( )	( )
7. Stone Container Corporation sells to various types of manufacturers. Mr. Stone's sales philosophy was, "When we found a smokestack, we knew we had a potential customer."	( )	( )	( )
8. Sales representatives for Caterpillar Tractor company use a detailed sales portfolio in their discussions with customers. This sales portfolio shows the Caterpillar tractors in use.	( )	( )	( )
9. By establishing an "800" phone line for their customers, Whirlpool, GE, and Polaroid were able to reduce warranty costs. Answering a telephone call·was estimated to cost one-half to one-third as much as responding to a letter.	( )	( )	( )
10. Ford Motor Co. is testing a Ford Selection Center Computer that provides automobile prospects with printouts on body styles, model availability and options without involving a salesperson. It was designed for dealerships selling 1,000 or more cars each year.	( )	( )	( )
11. Marketing military electronics, such as radar receivers, jammers, and decoys, involves anticipating Pentagon plans sometimes five years before a request for quotation. Prospective suppliers must gauge which Soviet electronics modifications most worry the Pentagon and must identify which military unit will be assigned responsibility for developing the system.	( )	( )	( )

Exercise 31-2   THE SELLING PROCESS

    Three major steps in the selling process are 1) pre-presentation,
2) presentation, and 3) follow-up. <u>Pre-presentation</u> includes the three
steps of prospecting, qualifying, and preapproach learning. Prospecting
is the process of identifying potential prospects. Qualifying is the process of screening prospects to see if they are worth pursuing further.
Preapproach learning is the process of learning about the prospect company
and its customers. <u>Presentation</u> includes the approach, the actual sales
presentation, any demonstration, handling objections, and efforts to close.
<u>Follow-up</u> includes checking to see that the product is delivered on time
and installed properly, as well as determining if the buyer is satisfied and
is using the purchased item properly.

        Instructions: Analyze each of the following statements
        and indicate which major step is involved. Select only
        one for each statement.

		Pre-presentation	Presentation	Follow-Up
1.	IBM sales representatives design their sales presentations to customers to fit the needs of the customer. This approach calls for the sales representative to have good listening and problem-solving skills.	( )	( )	( )
2.	Salespeople at Pittsburgh Brass Manufacturing Company in Irwin, Pennsylvania, use audiovisuals in their presentations to allow structured presentations with more uniform stressing of product features.	( )	( )	( )
3.	A college-book salesman was quite successful in getting college professors to adopt his company's textbooks. He would discover a professor's personal interest and approach him through that avenue.	( )	( )	( )
4.	A medical clinic specializes in minor plastic surgery. Each patient receives a personal phone call from the clinic approximately two weeks after surgery to check the progress of the patient.	( )	( )	( )

© 1986 by Prentice-Hall, A Division of Simon & Schuster, Inc.
Englewood Cliffs, N.J. 07632. All rights reserved.
Printed in the United States of America.

		Pre-presentation	Presentation	Follow-Up
5.	Penn Mutual Life Insurance Company suggests that its life-insurance agents qualify prospects on the basis of insurance need, ability to pay for the policy, and ability to qualify physically.	( )	( )	( )
6.	Norton's Abrasives Group prints a toll-free number in its advertisements. As a result, the salespeople are getting leads in three to four days rather than six or eight days.	( )	( )	( )
7.	National Cash Register salespeople are taught that they should try to close every sale at least seven times, if necessary.	( )	( )	( )
8.	Dow Chemical Company has national corporate accounts. Salespeople assigned to these key accounts continually check with their customers to see if the customers' orders are delivered on time.	( )	( )	( )
9.	"Companies no longer see complaints as a nuisance," according to TARP, Inc., a consumer-service consultant. "By providing an '800' telephone number, you can improve brand loyalty," according to TARP's president.	( )	( )	( )
10.	According to Doug Sanders, a golf pro, many business deals are made on a golf course. "When you sell a service, you first sell yourself. You play 18 holes and you really know a person."	( )	( )	( )
11.	Integrated Office Systems (IOS) offers business firms a computer-based integrated communications system that links field salespeople with home-office managers. At IOS, they first sell the concept. If the prospect is interested, IOS's applications specialists spend several days with salespeople to locate communications problems prior to designing a system.	( )	( )	( )

Exercise 31-3   THE SELLING PROCESS

Three major steps in the selling process are 1) pre-presentation, 2) presentation, and 3) follow-up. <u>Pre-presentation</u> includes the three steps of prospecting, qualifying, and preapproach learning. Prospecting is the process of identifying potential prospects. Qualifying is the process of screening prospects to see if they are worth pursuing further. Preapproach learning is the process of learning about the prospect company and its customers. <u>Presentation</u> includes the approach, the actual sales presentation, any demonstration, handling objections, and efforts to close. <u>Follow-up</u> includes checking to see that the product is delivered on time and installed properly, as well as determining if the buyer is satisfied and is using the purchased item properly.

Instructions: Analyze each of the following statements and indicate which major step is involved. Select only one for each statement.

	Pre-presentation	Presentation	Follow-Up
1. Many industrial-equipment sales representatives close their sales on minor points rather than the major equipment purchase decision.	( )	( )	( )
2. World Book Encyclopedia has developed a "canned" presentation for its salespeople. Each salesperson is expected to memorize and present this canned presentation to prospects.	( )	( )	( )
3. After installing new word processors, Micom Company salespeople revisit their customers and make sure the secretaries are using the word processors correctly.	( )	( )	( )
4. Schaevity Engineering is an industrial-instrumentation maker in New Jersey. Sales leads are provided to its sales reps that come from customers' inquiries about industrial ads. These inquiries are then analyzed on the basis of the inquiring firm and the product of interest.	( )	( )	( )
5. Corning Glass salesmen have a unique way to convince prospects that their glass is unbreakable. The salesmen	( )	( )	( )

© 1986 by Prentice-Hall, A Division of Simon & Schuster, Inc.
Englewood Cliffs, N.J. 07632. All rights reserved.
Printed in the United States of America.

let the prospect hit the glass with
a hammer.

6. American Express qualifies applicants ( ) ( ) ( )
for its credit card on the basis of
current income and job stability.
High-income applicants are encouraged
to obtain the American Express gold
card.

7. Venita Van Caspel owns a financial ( ) ( ) ( )
consulting firm in Houston. She
conducts free seminars on financial
planning which draw 400 to 500 interested people. These people become excellent prospects for her
financial services.

8. American Can produces machinery for ( ) ( ) ( )
the packaging needs of many indus-
tries. After installing new equipment, American Can sends a sales
engineer to the client for a month
to make sure the machinery is installed properly.

9. Exposition Management Group, a trade- ( ) ( ) ( )
exhibit consulting firm, suggests to
clients that they give out very
little literature at a trade fair
but concentrate on obtaining business cards so the clients' salespeople can visit the prospects'
office.

10. The National Office Products Asso- ( ) ( ) ( )
ciation,in cooperation with the
Wholesale Stationers Association,
are developing a joint procedure to
make possible the exchange of purchase orders and invoices over
phone lines between dealer, wholesaler and manufacturer computers.

11. When the Coca-Cola Co. changed its ( ) ( ) ( )
formula for Coke in 1985, it established a hotline, 1-800- GET COKE
to obtain consumer reaction.

Exercise 32-1   TYPES OF SALES POSITIONS

   Four major types of sales positions are 1) order taker , 2) tangible-
product seller , 3) intangible service seller , and 4) support personnel.
Order takers perform few selling functions besides taking orders or ringing up cash. Two types of order takers are inside order-takers and outside order-takers. Tangible-product sellers perform creative selling
functions for tangible products. These products can be sold to either
industrial or consumer buyers. Intangible-service sellers perform creative
selling functions for intangible services. Insurance, advertising, and
travel are types of intangible services. Support personnel perform non-
selling functions such as technical knowledge and better merchandising.
Support personnel includes sales engineers and missionary sales people.
Sales engineers help solve technical problems for industrial customers.
Missionary sales people perform promotional activities for manufacturers
or middlemen selling consumer products.

          Instructions: Analyze each of the following statements
          and indicate which sales position is described. Select
          only one for each statement.

		Order Takers	Tangible Product Sellers	Intangible Product Sellers	Support Personnel
1.	Addison-Wesley publishes col- lege textbooks. A 55-member sales force successfully intro- duced two new books in the nursing-school market.	( )	( )	( )	( )
2.	Gulf Oil Company has built a number of new self-service re- tail stations. The retail em- ployees clear the pumps and process the credit cards or collect the cash.	( )	( )	( )	( )
3.	Turner Broadcasting System in Atlanta pioneered the first "super-station," WTBS-TV. The salespeople have sold advertising to such large clients as Kellogg, Nestle, and Mercedes-Benz.	( )	( )	( )	( )
4.	Del Monte Corporation manufac- tures a wide line of food prod- ucts. In the sales department, a group of sales representatives work exclusively with retail store managers on shelf	( )	( )	( )	( )

© 1986 by Prentice-Hall, A Division of Simon & Schuster, Inc.
Englewood Cliffs, N.J. 07632. All rights reserved.
Printed in the United States of America.

	Order Takers	Tangible Product Sellers	Intangible Product Sellers	Support Personnel
management, displays, and other merchandising chores.				
5. Upjohn Pharmaceutical Company manufactures and sells a wide line of prescription drugs. The company salespeople are college graduates who spend their time calling on physicians and giving them information and free samples of their drug products.	( )	( )	( )	( )
6. Revco is a discount drug chain. The retail clerks work the cash registers and check out the customers for all products except prescription purchases.	( )	( )	( )	( )
7. Vice presidents from Chase Manhattan Bank in New York call on prospects and existing clients in many different types of industries.	( )	( )	( )	( )
8. Robert Tomize joined Xerox as a sales representative after finishing his MBA. He sells small copiers primarily to doctors, lawyers, and small businesses.	( )	( )	( )	( )
9. Complaints about retail service are becoming common. One customer of a major department store described the salespeople's duties as "they just take the money and see that people don't steal."	( )	( )	( )	( )
10. G. Neil Anderson sells about eight Apple computer systems a month in small towns in Idaho. He carries his samples in the trunk of his car. He calls on small businesses and farmers. He earned over $50,000 in 1984.	( )	( )	( )	( )

Exercise 32-2   TYPES OF SALES POSITIONS

Four major types of sales positions are 1) order takers, 2) tangible-product sellers, 3) intangible-service sellers, and 4) support personnel. <u>Order takers</u> perform few selling functions besides taking orders or ringing up cash. Two types of order takers are inside order takers and outside order-takers. <u>Tangible-product sellers</u> perform creative selling functions for tangible products. These products can be sold to either industrial or consumer buyers. <u>Intangible-service sellers</u> perform creative selling functions for intangible services. Insurance, advertising, and travel are types of intangible services. <u>Support personnel</u> perform non-selling functions such as technical knowledge and better merchandising. Support personnel includes sales engineers and missionary sales people. Sales engineers help solve technical problems for industrial customers. Missionary salespeople perform promotional activities for manufacturers or middlemen selling consumer products.

Instructions: Analyze each of the following statements and indicate which sales position is described. Select only one for each statement.

	Order Takers	Tangible Product Sellers	Intangible Product Sellers	Support Personnel
1. RCA has TV-service centers in many large metropolitan areas. The inside salespeople answer the telephone and dispatch repair personnel to the customers requesting TV service.	( )	( )	( )	( )
2. Russ Togs, Inc., is a diversified apparel maker that manufactures dresses, shirts, and sweaters. Forty-five sales reps in five regions sell to small retail accounts, as well as to the larger retail accounts.	( )	( )	( )	( )
3. Wonder Bread salespeople deliver bread daily to retail food stores and restaurants.	( )	( )	( )	( )
4. Mary Ellen Einstein is a sales representative for Hercules, Inc., of Delaware. She sells resin products to customers who make adhesives, coatings, and other industrial products.	( )	( )	( )	( )

© 1986 by Prentice-Hall, A Division of Simon & Schuster, Inc.
Englewood Cliffs, N.J. 07632. All rights reserved.
Printed in the United States of America.

	Order Takers	Tangible Product Sellers	Intangible Product Sellers	Support Personnel
5. R. J. Reynolds uses some of its sales personnel solely to work with its retailers to insure large displays, premium shelf space, and adequate stocking of its products.	( )	( )	( )	( )
6. Salespeople from the Marriott Hotel Corporation call on a variety of business accounts as well as soliciting convention business.	( )	( )	( )	( )
7. Metropolitan Life Insurance Company employs over 12,000 life-insurance agents to sell its various life-insurance policies.	( )	( )	( )	( )
8. Polyfiber Industries' plastic division manufactures and sells basic resins such as high-density polythylene, phenoxies, and styrenes. Under the district sales managers are a dozen applications engineers who give technical advice to end users of plastic products.	( )	( )	( )	( )
9. Digital Equipment Corp., which formerly hired electrical-engineering graduates to disseminate product knowledge to prospects, changed its policy in 1985 to hire experienced salespeople. This decision was made because of increased competition.	( )	( )	( )	( )
10. Don Love claims to have sold about 10% of the Cessna corporate jet aircraft although he does not work for Cessna. Mr. Love buys delivery positions on unbuilt Citation jets and later resells the positions at a profit to buyers who want to avoid the long wait for a new plane.	( )	( )	( )	( )

NAME _____

Exercise 32-3   TYPES OF SALES POSITIONS

Four major types of sales positions are 1) order takers, 2) tangible-product sellers, 3) intangible-service sellers, and 4) support personnel. <u>Order takers</u> perform few selling functions besides taking orders or ringing up cash. Two types of order takers are inside order takers and outside order takers. <u>Tangible-product sellers</u> perform creative selling functions for tangible products. These products can be sold to either industrial or consumer buyers. <u>Intangible-service sellers</u> perform creative selling functions for intangible services. Insurance, advertising, and travel are types of intangible services. <u>Support personnel</u> perform non-selling functions such as technical knowledge and better merchandising. Support personnel includes sales engineers and missionary sales people. Sales engineers help solve technical problems for industrial customers. Missionary salespeople perform promotional activities for manufacturers or middlemen selling consumer products.

Instructions: Analyze each of the following statements and indicate which sales position is described. Select only one for each statement.

	Order Takers	Tangible Product Sellers	Intangible Product Sellers	Support Personnel
1. Borden Company sells fresh milk to supermarkets in many areas of the country. Its salesmen deliver fresh milk every day and remove the milk that is out of date.	( )	( )	( )	( )
2. Retail clerks at Circle K convenience stores generally just check out customers at the cash register and stock empty shelves.	( )	( )	( )	( )
3. Armstrong-Cork Company sends out a sizable group of salespeople to work with their good retail accounts. These salespeople help retailers merchandise and display their products more effectively.	( )	( )	( )	( )
4. Jane Core sells advertising for McGraw-Hill's <u>Housing</u> magazine. Her mid-Atlantic sales this year are 82% ahead of last year's revenues.	( )	( )	( )	( )

© 1986 by Prentice-Hall, A Division of Simon & Schuster, Inc.
Englewood Cliffs, N.J. 07632. All rights reserved.
Printed in the United States of America.

	Order Takers	Tangible Product Sellers	Intangible Product Sellers	Support Personnel
5. Ryder Freight Company rents trucks to both businesses and consumers. The salesmen call on many firms who need temporary transportation.	( )	( )	( )	( )
6. Cessna Aircraft is the nation's leading maker of light airplanes. Salespeople calling on key corporate accounts provide prospects with a detailed travel analysis of their customary travel habits that increases sales of planes.	( )	( )	( )	( )
7. The Linde Division of Union Carbide Corp. sells waste water treatment systems to municipal and industrial markets. Its technical sales engineers work closely with clients in both the design and the installation stages.	( )	( )	( )	( )
8. Honeywell salesmen pursue multi-million-dollar contracts when they sell massive new computer systems to large companies and to federal and state agencies.	( )	( )	( )	( )
9. At Seattle-based Nordstrom department stores, salespeople are known for their high quality of service. They will obtain merchandise from other departments that they feel will match an item the prospect is considering.	( )	( )	( )	( )
10. E. F. Hutton's stockbroker Mark Olivari works the line of passenger cars stuck in traffic for ten minutes waiting to cross the Greater New Orleans Bridge. He says it is much more productive than contacting people on the telephone.	( )	( )	( )	( )
11. Most pharmaceutical manufacturers employ detailers who familiarize physicians and hospitals with the firms' newest products.	( )	( )	( )	( )

PART SIX

Managing the Marketing Effort

The hottest topic in business today is strategy. In this final section of the manual, the significant topic of competitive marketing strategy is addressed. Marketers must create strategies that best match organizational resources to environmental opportunities relevant to competitive behavior. The classification of competitive positions developed by Philip Kotler form the basis for the final set of exercises. Kotler points out that not only organizations but also their divisions and products can be classified by their behavior in an industry. The behavior can be that of a market leader, a market challenger, a market follower, or a market nicher.

Specific marketing behavioral strategies appear in Exercise 33. The student must analyze the specific behavior described and then decide under which classification it belongs. The student should realize that large organizations with a wide product line may use different competitive marketing strategies for different business units. What is significant is the situation being faced by that business unit. Two of the set of exercises are from a variety of situations; the third concentrates on the soft-drink industry, where the battles between Pepsico and the Coca-Cola Company are of interest to millions of consumers worldwide.

© 1986 by Prentice-Hall, A Division of Simon & Schuster, Inc.
Englewood Cliffs, N.J. 07632. All rights reserved.
Printed in the United States of America.

Exercise 33-1   COMPETITIVE STRATEGIES

Competitive strategies match company resources to environmental opportunities relative to the behavior of competitors. There are four behaviors
that apply. They are 1) market leader, 2) market challenger, 3) market
follower, and 4) market nicher. <u>Market-leader behavior</u> applies to the organization that has the largest market share and tries to increase the total
market by obtaining new users, new uses, and more usage. Brand prolifera-
ation is a major tool and continuous innovation is an offensive weapon.
<u>Market-challenger behavior</u> may apply to the second, third, or lower organi-
zation in the industry. This behavior involves aggressively attempting to
improve share position by attacking the leader, other runner-up firms, or
even smaller firms in the industry. <u>Market-follower behavior</u> reflects a
desire to be less aggressive than challengers, frequently following patterns
of conscious parallelism and avoiding competitive retaliation while maintaining growth. Individual strategies such as following the leader closely,
at a distance, or selectively are pursued. They frequently result in rates
of return that exceed the market leader. <u>Market-nicher behavior</u>, charac-
teristic of smaller organizations, involves specialization in serving small
segments frequently ignored by larger suppliers. This specialization may
involve end use, vertical level, customer size, geographic area, product,
or service feature, or quality.

Instructions: Read each of the following statements
and indicate the competitive strategy behavior involved. Select just one for each statement.

	Leader	Chal- lenger	Follower	Nicher
1. Executives at Marriott's Roy Rogers restaurant chain feel their major competitor in the quality niche of the fast-food market is Wendy's. RR shed its children's appeal in 1980 and introduced salad bars and cheese-burgers. Executives say "Wendy's is a national marketer with greater economies." Evaluate Roy Rogers.	( )	( )	( )	( )
2. Atlantic Richfield Co., the most price-competitive gasoline marketer, restructured its firm by discontin-uing its marketing operations east of the Mississippi river. It sold or closed over 2,000 service stations as well as its Philadelphia refinery.	( )	( )	( )	( )
3. After years of selling its equipment in the U.S. to other copier firms who resold Ricoh's products under their	( )	( )	( )	( )

© 1986 by Prentice-Hall, A Division of Simon & Schuster, Inc.
Englewood Cliffs, N.J. 07632. All rights reserved.
Printed in the United States of America.

own brand names, Ricoh Corp., one of
Japan's leading copier makers, has
targeted the U.S. as its most important market. It is expanding its
strategy to cover all product lines,
with an improved dealer network and
advertising. Since 1981 Ricoh's
sales of copiers have increased
tenfold.

4. "We have not broadened out of our   ( )   ( )   ( )   ( )
   specific area of the marketplace
   and have no intention of doing so,"
   the vice president-communications
   for Subaru said. In 1969, the firm
   concentrated in less competitive
   rural areas to get established. In
   the 1980's, it continued to emphasize
   four-wheel drive.

5. One of Beatrice Foods Co.'s many   ( )   ( )   ( )   ( )
   products is Country Line, a Mid-
   western brand of cheese. Rather
   than expanding nationwide where its
   $150,000 advertising budget would
   be dwarfed by advertising of industry leader Dart & Kraft, Country
   Line remains a profitable regional
   item.

6. In 1984, American Honda, in a major   ( )   ( )   ( )   ( )
   strategic change, announced plans to
   move into the upscale market then
   dominated by European auto makers like
   Audi and BMW. Its new car probably
   would not bear the Honda name and
   would not be sold through existing
   Honda dealers. The car would be
   larger and more expensive than
   existing Honda products.

7. When Procter & Gamble, market leader   ( )   ( )   ( )   ( )
   in soap and detergents, entered the
   cookie market with chewy soft-center
   Duncan Hines cookies in test,
   Nabisco responded immediately with
   two improved versions of Ship's Ahoy
   chocolate-chip cookies, and 18 varieties of a new line, Almost Home,
   also a soft-center cookie. Nabisco
   increased its market share 6 points
   to 40%.

212

Exercise 33-2   COMPETITIVE STRATEGIES

Competitive strategies match company resources to environmental opportunities relative to the behavior of competitors. There are four behaviors
that apply. They are 1) market leader, 2) market challenger, 3) market
follower, and 4) market nicher. <u>Market-leader behavior</u> applies to the organization that has the largest market share and tries to increase the total
market by obtaining new users, new uses, and more usage. Brand prolifera-
ation is a major tool and continuous innovation is an offensive weapon.
<u>Market-challenger behavior</u> may apply to the second, third, or lower organi-
zation in the industry. This behavior involves aggressively attempting to
improve share position by attacking the leader, other runner-up firms, or
even smaller firms in the industry. <u>Market-follower behavior</u> reflects a
desire to be less aggressive than challengers, frequently following patterns
of conscious parallelism and avoiding competitive retaliation while maintaining growth. Individual strategies such as following the leader closely,
at a distance, or selectively are pursued. They frequently result in rates
of return that exceed the market leader. <u>Market-nicher behavior</u>, charac-
teristic of smaller organizations, involves specialization in serving small
segments frequently ignored by larger suppliers. This specialization may
involve end use, vertical level, customer size, geographic area, product
or service feature, or quality.

Instructions: Read each of the following statements
and indicate the competitive strategy behavior involved. Select just one for each statement.

	Leader	Chal- lenger	Follower	Nicher
1. In 1982, Black & Decker had 20% of the worldwide professional tool mar- ket. Japan's Makita Electric Works Ltd., and other Japanese tool companies captured an equivalent amount. Al- though B&D was unable that year to match the Japanese firms' production costs, B&D matched competitors' price cuts.	( )	( )	( )	( )
2. Milwaukee Electric Tool Corp., a division of Amstar Corp. sells a much more expensive line of tools than Black & Decker and Makita in the U.S. Milwaukee feels it has not been directly challenged by the Japanese and has not cut prices.	( )	( )	( )	( )
3. Chaparral Steel Co. is a new, non- union specialty steel mill. It pays labor about half the traditional	( )	( )	( )	( )

© 1986 by Prentice-Hall, A Division of Simon & Schuster, Inc.
Englewood Cliffs, N.J. 07632. All rights reserved.
Printed in the United States of America.

steelworker rates and produces a
ton of steel with an average of two
man hours compared with large U.S.
mills' average of five-to-eight
and Japan's 2.8. Chaparral competes on price by restricting itself to construction steel only.

4. Shortly after its introduction,   ( )   ( )   ( )   ( )
Procter & Gamble's Crest toothpaste
became the industry's best seller.
In 1969 and again in 1975, Lever
Brothers worked to reduce Crest's
lead by successfully marketing
sweet-flavored gels.

5. Procter & Gamble's Charmin is the top   ( )   ( )   ( )   ( )
selling brand of toilet paper in the
U.S. P&G continues to test market
new brands Certain, Banner and Summit.
The latter two brands are aimed at
the generic and private-label tis-
sue that account for 30% of the
market.

6. Despite vigorous competition from   ( )   ( )   ( )   ( )
Burger King, Wendy's, and others,
McDonald's Corp. sells 4.35 billion
burgers a year through 8,000 restaurants in 31 countries. Fish
sandwiches were added in 1963, Egg
McMuffins in 1973, breakfasts in
1977, Chicken McNuggets in 1983,
and salad bars in 1984.

7. One of every two large trucks   ( )   ( )   ( )   ( )
in the U.S. is powered by a Cummins
diesel engine. General Motors Corp.
is second in the industry. Cummins
is also active in the lower-
horsepower market making farm, construction, and industrial engines as
well as small bus engines. Its
large industrial diesels power off-
shore drilling rigs.

8. Procter & Gamble had a 75% share of   ( )   ( )   ( )   ( )
the disposable-diaper market prior to
Kimberly-Clark's successful introduction of its Huggies premium diaper.
KC made a significant improvement
over P&G's Pampers, reducing Pamper's
share to less than 50%.

214

Exercise 33-3   COMPETITIVE STRATEGIES

Competitive strategies match company resources to environmental opportunities relative to the behavior of competitors. There are four behaviors
that apply. They are 1) market leader, 2) market challenger, 3) market
follower, and 4) market nicher. <u>Market-leader behavior</u> applies to the organization that has the largest market share and tries to increase the total
market by obtaining new users, new uses, and more usage. Brand prolifera-
ation is a major tool and continuous innovation is an offensive weapon.
<u>Market-challenger behavior</u> may apply to the second, third, or lower organi-
zation in the industry. This behavior involves aggressively attempting to
improve share position by attacking the leader, other runner-up firms, or
even smaller firms in the industry. <u>Market-follower behavior</u> reflects a
desire to be less aggressive than challengers, frequently following patterns
of conscious parallelism and avoiding competitive retaliation while maintaining growth. Individual strategies such as following the leader closely,
at a distance, or selectively are pursued. They frequently result in rates
of return that exceed the market leader. <u>Market-nicher behavior</u>, charac-
teristic of smaller organizations, involves specialization in serving small
segments frequently ignored by larger suppliers. This specialization may
involve end use, vertical level, customer size, geographic area, product
or service feature, or quality.

> Instructions: Read each of the following statements
> and indicate the competitive strategy behavior in-
> volved. Select just one for each statement.

	Leader	Chal-lenger	Follower	Nicher
1. Aiming at Seven-Up, PepsiCo intro-duced Slice, a lightly carbonated lemon-lime with 10% fruit juice in 1985. Some resistance by PepsiCo bottlers was observed because ap-proximately 20% of them handled Seven-Up.	( )	( )	( )	( )
2. When consumption growth for soft drinks slowed to 3% annually in 1982, down from the 6% increase ten years earlier, Coca-Cola Co. began adding a stream of new products. They included Diet Coke, Caffeine-free Coke, Caffeine-free Diet Coke, Caffeine-free Tab, Minute Maid Orange soda, and Cherry Coke. Cola-Cola also added new package sizes ranging up to a gigantic 3-liter bottle. Coke now has 18 drinks in more than 100 packages.	( )	( )	( )	( )

© 1986 by Prentice-Hall, A Division of Simon & Schuster, Inc.
Englewood Cliffs, N.J. 07632. All rights reserved.
Printed in the United States of America.

	Leader	Challenger	Follower	Nicher

3. Dr. Pepper Co. ranks third in the soft-drink industry with about a 7% share. Its president says, "I'm not about to get into a slugging contest with Coke and Pepsi." Many of its bottlers also bottle a cola such as Pepsi or Coke. ( ) ( ) ( ) ( )

4. Although Cola-Cola Co.'s Tab was the best-selling diet cola, Coke's research indicted Tab appealed most to calorie-conscious females of above-average education. Because research showed that men would be receptive to a low-calorie approach, Diet Coke, featuring bold, red graphics was introduced nationally with a huge promotional budget. ( ) ( ) ( ) ( )

5. The soft-drink industry can be divided many ways. One classification identifies price. The national brands such as Coke, Pepsi, 7 Up, and RC have traditionally been the highest priced. Lowest have been supermarkets' private brands. In between have been warehouse brands such as Shasta, which are delivered through the grocery distribution system rather than by a company route salesperson. Evaluate Shasta, which has a modest promotional budget yet wide distribution. ( ) ( ) ( ) ( )

6. H. M. O'Neill, a major Seven-Up and RC bottler, feels the only way small firms can survive against Coke and Pepsi is through segmentation. ( ) ( ) ( ) ( )

7. Chicago-based A. J. Canfield developed Canfield's Diet Chocolate Fudge soda. It was so popular that store managers volunteered to put up the displays. ( ) ( ) ( ) ( )

8. Ever since 1966, when Coca-Cola Co. franchised a bottler in Israel, many Middle Eastern countries have boycotted Coke. Double Cola has moved into Oman, Qatar, and the United Arab Emirates. Foreign sales are now about 20% of Double Cola's sale. ( ) ( ) ( ) ( )

Non-Quantitative Set

Exercise No.	1st Column	2nd Column	3rd Column	4th Column	5th Column	6th Column
1-1	1,2,6	5,8,9	3,7	4,10		
2-1	4,6,9,12	1,7,8,10	2,3,5,11			
3-1	1,6,11	3,9,10,15	4,7,8,14	2,5,12,13		
5-1	1,2	8,9,11	4,6,7	3,5,10		
6-1	4,6,9	1,2	3,5	7,8		
7-1	9,10	1,4,11	13	2,6	3,7,12	5,8,14
8-1	2,6	8,9	3,7	1,5	4,10	
9-1	1,3,7	4,5,6,8	2,9			
10-1	4,7	1,8	3,6	2,5,9		
11-1	4,7	2,5,8,10	1,3,6,9			
13-1	4,7,8,11,13	2,6,9,14	1,3,5,10,12			
14-1	4,5,8	9,11,12	1,3,10	2,6,7		
15-1	2,5,8,11	1,3,6,12	4,7,9,10			
16-1	2,3,7,9,11,12	1,5,8,10	4,6,13			
17-1	4,7	2,6	1,5	3		
19-1	1,6,8	2,5,7,10	3,4,9,11			
20-1	1,2,3,8,10,11	4,5,6,7,9,12				
21-1	2,6,10,12	4,7,9	3,8	1,5,11		
23-1	2,4,5,6,11	1,3,7,8,9,10				
24-1	4,6,8,10	2,5,9,11	1,3,7			
25-1	1,5,7	3,6,9,10,11	2,4,8			
26-1	5,6,8	2,4,9,10	1,3,7			
28-1	7,8,11	1,6	2,4,10	3,5,9		
29-1	5,7,9	3,6	1	2,4,8		
30-1	2,4,5,8,9	1,3,6,7,10				
31-1	1,4,7,10,11	5,6,8	2,3,9			
32-1	2,6,9	1,8,10	3,7	4,5		
33-1	7	1,3,6	5	2,4		

© 1986 by Prentice-Hall, A Division of Simon & Schuster, Inc.
Englewood Cliffs, N.J. 07632. All rights reserved.
Printed in the United States of America.

Quantitative Set

4-1   Relative Market Share   Relative Market Growth

(C)	1.107		8%
(P)	0.938		6
(L)	0.5		6
(T)	2.75		4

12-1   1)

			2)		
Sales	$11,000,000		Sales	$10,400,000	
Contribution	2,500,000		Contribution	2,600,000	
Net Profit	300,000		Net Profit	400,000	

18-1   1)

			2)		
Sales	$ 1,250		Sales	$ 1,750	
Contribution	1,125		Contribution	1,500	
Net Profit	(375)		Net Profit	-0-	

18-5

List price of items sold	$1,000
Final users price (25% off list)	750
Price to electrical contractors (40% off list)	600
Price to wholesalers (40% and 10%)	540
Price to manufacturers' agents (10% of $540)	54
Revenue to Vestal Products Inc.	486

18-6

TC	$50,000	$51,000	$52,000	$53,000	$54,000
TFC	50,000	50,000	50,000	50,000	50,000
TVC	0	1,000	2,000	3,000	4,000
AC	-	51,000	26,000	17,667	13,500
AFC	-	50,000	25,000	16,000	12,000
AVC	-	1,000	1,000	1,000	1,000

22-1

Sales	$16,500,000
Contribution	5,900,000
Net Profit	3,900,000

22-4   1) $1,500,000   2) $250,000   3) 3.3%

      4) 12.5%   5) $400,000

27-1   1)

Sales	$27,000,000	2)	1,000,000 case sales
Contribution	10,800,000	3)	1,333,383 case sales
Net Profit	2,800,000		

27-5

A	50	30	$1,333	$48,000
B	42	50	1,250	30,000
C	100	55	833	50,000
D	112.5	77	900	108,000
E	150	80	1,125	54,000
Average	91	58	$1,088	$58,000

Two best: D,E   Two worst: A,B

NOTES

NOTES

NOTES

NOTES

NOTES

NOTES

NOTES

NOTES